Invest In
Apartment Buildings

Profit Without The Pitfalls

Invest In Apartment Buildings

Profit Without The Pitfalls

THERESA BRADLEY-BANTA

Big Fish Top Dogs Publishing

Cover and book design by: Bradley Banta Design

ISBN 978-0-9859681-0-6

FIRST EDITION

Library of Congress Control Number: 2012918795

Big Fish Top Dogs Publishing
3570 E. 12th Ave.
Denver, CO 80206
www.bigfishtopdogs.com

Printed in U.S.A.

Dedication

To Richard,
for being the best husband a girl could ask for.

Contents

Preface

I fell in love with real estate investing in 2004 when my husband and I realized that we could purchase a beautiful 1890 Victorian home then keep our former home as a cash flowing residential rental property. The best part is that we actually lowered our monthly expenses significantly (we even moved our two offices home saving thousands a year!). And so began my real estate investing journey, including working with extraordinary real estate business mentors.

Since then, investing in residential real estate, including multifamily properties and apartment buildings, has become a 24/7 preoccupation. It's a marriage of my two passions: mentoring and growing wealth through the acquisition of appreciating assets. I've invested successfully across the United States and in Mexico and I've consistently doubled my net worth throughout the years.

But what stands out is that along the way I've put much of my time and energy into teaching others—from beginners to professional real estate investors with millions—how to be wise investors without following what is often the incorrect advice of the "gurus" of the moment. The key to success in real estate investing is to get the best possible education/mentorship without the hype.

From these roots come this book. Enjoy it and if you need sound advice, please visit my website at www.theresabradleybanta.com. You will find free downloads from this book. Please take advantage of them; and feel free to email me with any questions you have or educational information that you need. I look forward to having you join me on this journey.

Acknowledgments

My deepest thanks to the people I spend time with in the trenches. This book would not exist without you.

Richard. You always bring me back down to earth even when I'm certain the sky is falling. So far it hasn't. And if it does? I've got you. You are the best man in the world to be with through thick and thin.

My mentor Steve Parker. You taught me that deal making is an art form. I think of you every time I leave something on the table for the other guy. You were worth every penny.

My coach Will for getting me into action.

My favorite broker Bob. I hope you don't mind that I changed your name. Thanks for sticking with me through thick and thin. You're smart and you know how to listen.

Mom. Thanks for raising me to believe I could do anything I put my heart to. And thanks for the edits—I'm sure I will always be the comma queen in your mind when you think of this book.

Janet. Masterminding with you has been a blast.

And last but not least, my team, partners, colleagues and mentoring clients. Thank you.

—Theresa Bradley-Banta

Introduction

Steve White read *all* the books on investing in apartment buildings. He paid $5,000 to attend a three-day multifamily investing seminar. At the close of the seminar he spent *another* $3,795 at the back of the room for software and a home study workbook with DVDs. After this considerable investment of time and money, Steve couldn't figure out why he was paralyzed with fear, self-doubt and apprehension.

He was frustrated beyond belief. The multifamily real estate gurus he was reading and following promised, "Investing in real estate is fast and easy money—anyone can do it!" He should be well on his way to making millions in real estate, shouldn't he? Steve's wife, who was already dubious about his intent to go out and buy an apartment building, told him, "Steve, you know, maybe it's time for you to give up this dream and keep your day job after all."

Steve's story is a common one. After an investment of thousands of dollars, Steve felt stuck. He had learned to use fancy multifamily investing software; in fact he now owned some. Nevertheless he still wasn't sure he knew how to tell a good deal from a bad one. Heck, he wasn't sure if he knew how to *find* a good deal—even if he knew the good from the bad. For instance, should he start with small deals and work his way up? Could he really raise the money for his first deal? Was his wife right after all? Maybe he should just give it up before he lost all of his money, and, since he was looking for investors, all of his friend's and family's money, too.

Steve realized he wasn't sure where to go for help. And now he began wondering if the rumors he was hearing were true. That the real estate investing boot camp he just attended was nothing but an opportunity for the "guru" to upsell him into other products. The guru was richer but Steve didn't feel independently wealthy or free. Maybe none of this was real. Maybe the opportunity to earn millions in multifamily real estate was a big fiction.

The "gurus" referred to in this book are the self-styled real estate "experts" who work tirelessly to sell programs but spend very little time giving their students a *reality based* multifamily investing education. The promises of easy money and no work are designed to line the pockets of the so-called gurus. I wrote this book because I want you to know what will work and what will help you be a successful real estate investor.

Invest In Apartment Buildings *Profit Without The Pitfalls* is full of the stories the real estate gurus hope you never learn. It sheds light on the "surefire strategies" the real estate gurus promote. It debunks the often-misguided advice potential investors hear and read as they follow these industry "experts."

This book changes that. Through stories derived from my actual in-the-street experiences you will gain real *and actionable* knowledge about investing in multifamily real estate. You'll learn how to tell a good deal from a bad one, negotiate like a pro, pick the right market and hire a *great* team.

By the way, all of the exhibits, documents and forms used in this book and in the Appendix are available for (free) download at www. theresabradleybanta.com/bookdownloads.

CHAPTER ONE

✳

*It's tangible, it's solid, it's beautiful. It's artistic, from my
standpoint, and I just love real estate.*
—Donald Trump

Ownership Benefits

There is a caveat for this chapter before we jump in. I get right into
the challenges of investing in apartment buildings. I leave no stone
unturned. I do so because I want you to be fully informed on all
aspects of this exciting investment. The good, the bad and the ugly.
There are some horror stories. Stories that may make you sit back
in your chair and think, "Whoa! Not so fast! Maybe I don't want to
invest in multifamily properties."

You know what? That's exactly what I want you to think.

I want you to think long and hard about the fact that buying an apartment building is more like buying a business and a lot less like investing in real estate. You can do many things wrong if you leap blindly

into multifamily real estate investing. You can lose hundreds of hours of sleep, your "sanity" and all of your money.

Throughout this book, I'll give you techniques for investing the smart way. I'll show you shortcuts that will actually limit your potential for mistakes and save you a great deal of time.

As you read the stories I believe your confidence and excitement will soar. At the end you'll find yourself saying "Yes, I can do this!" With good education and mentoring, you can do everything right. Sure, you might make little mistakes here and there but that's how you learn.

Horror stories? Okay, my husband says that's a little strong. Even though he has personally lived through some of these stories.

How about "nightmares"? That term might be more appropriate. After all it's the nightmares that keep you awake at night wondering things like:

- What am I going to do about this structural issue that suddenly appeared?
- Why did we go from a building that was almost full to a 73% occupancy? Practically overnight? How will I make the mortgage payment?
- How am I going to get my manager to put great tenants in my property?
- How am I going to fire my manager when I don't even have a good replacement?
- How long will my reserve funds last while I turn the property around?

There's nothing like a great success story to make these nightmares seem like something barely remembered in the past. But why even live through them? Education, good planning and great exit strategies can keep nightmares to a minimum.

That's what this book is all about. It will help you go into multifamily investing with your eyes wide open—*and keep the mistakes to a minimum.*

The Advantages of Multifamily Real Estate

Multifamily real estate has many advantages over other real estate asset classes (such as single-family, industrial, retail and office). There is no disagreement with real estate gurus on this point.

On paper and in the classroom, the list of advantages to buying apartment buildings looks great. You have:

- Creative deal structuring and financing.
- Less competition: Apartment investing is the market "Sweet Spot."
- Stable, predictable cash flow.
- Professional third party property management.
- Multiple profit sources: Cash flow, appreciation, numerous tax deductions & benefits and principle pay down.
- Benefits from economies of scale.

But it's when you actually get in the trenches that you discover pretty ideas and broad, sweeping generalizations may not be easy to accomplish or even put into practice. Be aware of the fact that while there may be many advantages to buying commercial real estate, you can still get hurt if you don't know what you're doing. If it were easy, like following a recipe, everyone would be doing it. The real estate gurus will try to get you to believe that all you need to do is buy the list of ingredients, follow the directions, and you'll have a perfect dish every time.

In this chapter we'll take a look at these various advantages from a very realistic point of view. I want to be sure you don't buy the guru's sales pitch hook, line and sinker.

Small Buildings May Not Cover Professional Management

I'll agree it's a wonderful thing having an investment property that can financially swing paying for professional third party management. That means you are not answering the phone in the middle of the night because a tenant's toilet overflows—you have a manager handling this and similar problems for you.

You've heard these stories right? "I got into buying apartment buildings because I didn't want to be a landlord. I just wanted to sit back and collect the rents." The gurus entice a lot of new investors into apartment deals based on this *single* statement alone. Yet many properties don't produce enough cash to afford professional management for a number of reasons.

Small apartment buildings (50 units or less) generally do not produce enough cash flow for you to pay a third party manager and afford to pay yourself a monthly distribution at the same time. If you've financed your deal and you do not have a lot of equity in the property, the cash profit margins can be small or non-existent. A general rule of thumb is that complexes that are over 50 units in size will support third party management. Of course a way to get around this is to own multiple properties in the same area which total more than 50 units.

When you contemplate getting into multifamily investing you'll have to ask yourself some questions. What is my investment strategy? Am I okay with being a landlord for the first few years of my investment journey? The next 5-10 years? The answers will depend on how fast you grow your portfolio of properties.

Depending on your investment strategy, which we'll cover in greater detail later, you may have to give serious consideration as to whether or not you want to be a property manager at all.

I know a guy who invested in the neighborhood of $7,000 in a real estate boot camp only to decide he didn't want to invest in apartment buildings after all. He didn't want to spend the hours it would require to be a successful apartment investor. The caution here is to be careful about what you hear—and about what you buy into.

Real estate is a business. And if you want to succeed you need to treat it as a business.

Real estate is a business.

Are you buying an investment property or are you actually buying yourself a job? The answer depends on the type of property you buy, your investment strategy, and your team. If your property is less than 50 units, chances are you will be the manager *or* you can take the property cash flow and pay someone else to manage for you—by forfeiting any cash flow for yourself.

7

In short, not all properties will generate enough income to allow you to hire a manager. Your expenses may be too high. You may have collection problems with your tenants. You may be in a neighborhood that the best management companies will not work in.

I've seen it happen.

The good news? By properly screening your deals and markets and by negotiating good prices and terms on those deals, you can get a system in place where you are not the manager. It will depend on your team and on the terms of your deal.

I generally have professional managers managing my properties. It's great in that I don't deal with residents at my properties. I walk the properties and the residents know and recognize me but I do not lease units or take maintenance calls. However with some properties, the margins can be really thin.

Great Property Managers Are Hard to Find

Let's suppose you buy a property that can afford to pay for a manager and give you a monthly cash flow at the same time. Multifamily managers will screen and lease units to your tenants. They will handle all of the maintenance issues on a timely basis (by the way, most tenants think "timely" means yesterday). A manager will handle the books—collect the rents, pay the bills, keep a Balance Sheet, a General Ledger, a Cash Flow Statement and a Rent Roll.

Some of the very worst stories I can tell you as an apartment building owner revolve around my highly qualified (on paper they look great) management companies taking their eyes off the ball. I promise you, when this stuff was going on I was not sitting back watching the distribution checks roll in. I had serious income and management issues to deal with not to mention nightmares.

The Hot Shot Owner, Operator, Manager and His Woes

We had the owner of a professional management company handling one of our properties. Let's call him Larry. I hired him because he was currently the owner and operator of multiple apartment buildings in the area. He had approximately 150 units that he personally owned and managed. Plus he was a third-party manager for 12-15 other local properties. He thought like an owner. In other words he:

- Was great at increasing property income, especially in areas often overlooked by less experienced managers.
- Knew how to lower expenses—and keep them down.
- Was adept at renovating properties without going hog wild on unnecessary upgrades.
- Understood the market sizzle that rented properties.

As you read this book, you, too will learn to think like an owner.

For a while Larry did a great job for us. We were getting fantastic renters. Our vacancies were at market if not lower. Renovations were underway and we were staying within our budget. We also had an on-site manager, Rob, who traded rent for minor maintenance work. He also received fees for leasing units to new tenants and for renewing the leases of existing tenants. Rob was the face of the property and the residents loved him.

Then all hell broke loose.

Larry's sister, who lived out of state, became terminally ill. Suddenly Larry was rarely at the property and he stopped managing the renovation and maintenance teams.

At the same time, he decided to buy two new properties for himself— properties that needed a ton of work. Throughout this time, Larry professed loudly that he was on the job and none of these extracurricular activities would take him away from our property.

And then the final straw. Rob, the on-site manager who was loved by all, decided to move overseas.

In a single month's time we went from a 7% vacancy to over 25%. Our timely maintenance and renovations stopped dead in their tracks. The residents moved out in droves.

While none of this was intentional, the ultimate problem was that Larry did not have enough team to handle his unforeseen changing circumstances. He didn't have a second in command with the know-how to step in—someone who could immediately hire an on-site manager to replace Rob and take over the management of the maintenance teams. And he picked an unfortunate time to acquire more properties for his own portfolio.

There's no question Larry took his eyes off the ball. Yet as an owner, I had to realize that I am the ultimate manager of my assets. We fired Larry. His problems could not become our problems.

There is a silver lining to this story. I learned a lot from Larry. His knowledge as an owner of apartment buildings was priceless. For quite a while there he was a great mentor—in fact, all of my best real estate mentors have been owners of multifamily properties.

The Non-Owner Operator Manager and His Ego

Then there are the managers that don't own any properties personally. The very ones that love to tell you how much they know. Rarely have I seen non-owner operators do a stellar job managing other people's deals. They simply don't—or can't—think like owners of multi-unit properties. (In fact, some of the property owners I know don't think that way either. I'm going to make sure you do!)

Unfortunately, I've had my share of this type of property manager on my team. And I've found their learning curves can be high. I think income. These managers think—well, I don't know what they think sometimes. For example, I've had a non-owner manager tell me in his weekly report, "We leased two units this week."

And I ask, "That's it?"

Here's the thing. I'm not unhappy with the fact he leased two units. It's what he didn't tell me. I want to know:

- How much did each unit rent for?
- What were the lease terms? One year? Six months?
- Did he offer concessions in order to rent the unit (such as one month free rent or a discounted deposit)?
- Did the tenant lease a storage unit?
- Did they lease one of the designated parking spaces?

- Are they now on our utility reimbursement program?

I do not want to drag this information out of my property managers. As I said, an owner "gets" that it's all about income. Every dime or dollar counts. A twenty-dollar a month parking space (times 30 or 50 residents) adds up. When the manager overlooks these resources, he's completely missed additional opportunities for income. You'd be surprised at how many times you have to drill this into the heads of non-owner managers. Income. Income. Income. They get it—but they don't always put the knolwedge into practice.

> **As I said, an owner "gets" that it's all about income. Every dime or dollar counts.**

So, are you still ready to believe the gurus—carte blanche? I know you'll think twice the next time you hear them say, "Owning apartment buildings is a *beautiful thing*. You'll never have to manage a property. You just collect the rent and it's a happy, happy day." This is true only when you have top notch managers working for you.

In a perfect world, things go smoothly. But awesome property managers are hard to find. They can be hard to keep. They may not think like you do. They must be considered as one of the most key and valuable members of your team because they are but it's *your* job to be sure they perform.

Self-Managed Mom and Pop Buildings

Some owners actually like to keep rents below market and manage the property themselves. These are deals where the owner has a lot of equity in the property and can afford to keep income lower. In other words, the property debt has been paid down significantly and the owner is getting a pretty decent cash flow.

I see a lot of what are commonly referred to as "Mom and Pop" buildings where the owner has only one property—purchased as a retirement investment. These are properties that will have only one owner for decades. By keeping rents below market, the owner tends to keep long-term tenants which fits perfectly with the long-term hold approach. When you've got long-term happy residents most of the management duties are minimized and it becomes a fairly easy property to manage.

However, if you buy a highly leveraged apartment deal, with very little equity going in, the cash flow on the property is going to be severely limited because your mortgage payments (debt service) will be high. You'll need to get every dime you can in rents and other income to stay in black numbers (positive cash flow).

Now let's discuss another advantage to owning commercial property. This, too, is a hot item the gurus love to talk about.

Stable, Predictable Cash Flow

If you are not tired of the management stories I can think of another one that highlights how the search for stable and predictable cash flow can backfire.

It's true that multifamily properties, by the sheer of volume of renters, provide a more stable and predictable cash flow over a lot of other real estate classes, especially more than single-family properties. If you are the owner of a single-family rental property, then you know the loss of a tenant can mean the loss of your entire cash flow on that property for the year.

With an apartment building, allowing for expected vacancies and turnover, you can predict your annual income on the property with pretty good accuracy—especially if you have a great management team in place (or are doing a great job yourself keeping the property full and you are collecting timely rent payments).

But what if you have collection problems at your property? And what if your management team doesn't get a handle on it? The minute a tenant gets into trouble paying rent on time (and the minute you let it continue) you can be looking at a serious problem.

And it can snowball and get even worse. If one tenant pays late, the entire apartment community can follow suit. Word gets around.

We had a manager who let collections become a problem. Tenants were falling two and three months behind in rent payments. In order to "fix" it, he started renting to Coalition for the Homeless (CCH) residents against our directions. We okayed two new subsidized residents. He leased to nine. He did it because the rents were federally guaranteed, they were paid at the beginning of each and every month, and—ta da!—his collection problems were at an end.

Leasing to subsidized tenants made the job easy for him—but (speaking of nightmares earlier) this became an almost instant disaster for us. Apartment communities are just that. They are "communities." One bad tenant can influence the entire population. Some of the new

CCH residents were truly great—I remember one guy whose unit looked like it was right out of house beautiful—but others had literally been saved from the streets and they brought the streets into our halls and apartment units. Drug deals. Guns. All night parties.

Drug deals. Guns. All night parties. Attack dogs.

Attack dogs. Bed bugs. Visits from the cops. And guess what? One and all of these new tenants were on one-year leases. Worse? The CCH leases trumped ours. We were stuck.

We lost some good tenants during the time it took to get the bad tenants out. We had unforeseen and unbudgeted expenses in the form of expensive pest control treatments. Can you see how what might have been "stable and predictable" cash flow became highly unpredictable?

With good management it is generally possible to have stable and predictable cash flow. The more aware you are of the potential pitfalls, the better you can be at managing a great asset. Here's where you can be proactive:

- Carefully instruct and monitor your management team on who you want in your community. Put it in writing.
- Keep a careful watch on expenses and rising costs. It's a great idea to interview market vendors annually (service providers such as trash hauling companies, laundry leasing services, landscaping and snow removal, maintenance, pest control, insurance, telephone, security, etc.). Let your current vendors know you will do annual shopping for services.
- Keep a careful watch on rent collections.
- Keep an eye on what your market is doing in terms of

average vacancies and make sure your management team is leasing at market standards.

- Track the market rents and concessions (if any) of all your competitors. Can you increase rent? Do you need to be more competitive?
- Be creative about offering concessions. For example, I like to offer three months free parking (or storage) rather than a cut in rent for new tenants. After three months, they become used to the idea of designated parking and chances are they will continue to pay for the privilege. With discounted rent payments, again you're stuck.

By far, having a great management team in place, or doing a stellar job as a manager yourself is the key to your success as an apartment building owner.

Let's look at some of the other advantages as presented by the gurus.

Appreciation: The Gurus Will Tell You To Count on It

I've heard top multifamily gurus insist you can raise the rents on tenants once per year. And that as rents are raised, the value of the property goes up. They'll also tell you that as you pay down your mortgage, your equity increases.

In a perfect world this thinking may hold true. But we all know about the Great Recession.

Rents can and will go down. It happens in a poor economy and it happens in normal real estate market cycles, too.

Rents can have downward pressure on them if your market becomes saturated with available, and similar, rental units. Shadow markets such as rental single-family properties can suddenly flood the market and compete with your apartment units.

Equity can disappear overnight if property values plunge. Your acquisition strategies are key. We will be discussing these strategies throughout the book. Buying your property for the right price *going in* is critical. I'm sure you've heard this before: "You must make your money on real estate at the time you do the deal."

The good news is you can plan for these contingencies by having a solid strategy in place before you do your first deal. Reading this book is an excellent place to start.

Let's look at yet another selling point the gurus love to promote. If you are a student of the industry, I know you've seen the pitches about doing wildly creative deals and buying properties with no money down. But is it true?

Creative Deal Structuring and Financing

If you love to negotiate, you'll love investing in apartment complexes. Most owners, brokers and lenders understand negotiation is part of the process, both when you buy and when you sell. But beware. You'll find much information in the market and online about how you can find a hundred ways to buy a property with no money down. I love reading about them—I've even brought some of those ideas to the negotiating table. But many of them are pretty far-fetched. For instance, asking your commercial broker to "loan" their commission to you to help with your down payment in exchange for interest payments on their loan. Very few, if any, brokers will bite. Or, for example, the so called "subject to" deal where the seller deeds the property to you but keeps the *existing* mortgage in place. This is extremely high risk. If the current lender discovers this type of transaction they may actually exercise their Due on Sale Clause and demand the note be paid off in full.

Creative deals are not exclusive to apartment buildings. Most everything is negotiable. When the gurus tell you this is exclusive to buying apartment buildings, don't believe it.

I recently asked a top lender in apartment buildings (for our market) out to coffee. When I asked her, "What are some of the most creative deals you've done recently?" she answered with a flat, "We don't *do* creative deals." Huh? She represents a huge institutional lender—and they don't do creative deals. According to her lending is so tight on apartment deals, her underwriting department rarely approves loans with creative deal structuring.

This is simply food for thought. Sometimes the hype gets out of control. The gurus want you to think you can waltz in and buy an apartment building with none of your own money—and do it in 100 different ways! In reality most of these "no money down, no money out of your pocket" strategies are a stretch. It's great to go for them, but don't bank on wild strategies working every time you do a deal.

Sometimes the hype gets out of control.

Next on my guru hype list is:

Multifamily Properties Offer Economies of Scale

Now, this is a general statement I actually agree with—for the most part. Handling improvements, marketing, management, and repositioning for example on a single apartment building as opposed to, say, 12 single-family houses definitely has its advantages.

I recently met a guy at a real estate convention. He mentioned after learning that I invest in multifamily complexes that he had a 10-unit property for sale. Then he told me that it was actually spread over eight properties. It was a mix of detached units and duplexes. He was a little bit surprised when I said that I really had no interest in pursuing the deal because I didn't want a property with eight furnaces, eight roofs, eight air conditioning systems, etc.

When you buy an apartment building you have one roof, one boiler, one common area, one lawn, one air conditioning system, one security system. Single, rather than multiple, systems make economic sense—especially when dealing with maintenance and repair costs. Replacement costs are lower with a smaller quantity of mechanicals. And it's easier to market and manage a single property—for example, advertising costs are lower with one property; rental showings are conducted at one location (you are not driving all over town showing multiple properties); and your tenants are all under one roof.

On the flip side, especially when it comes to renovations, you've got to know what you're doing. If you have misconceived notions of property upgrades, the economies of scale can break your budget. I know investors who have renovated the units in their buildings to condo quality standards. They put in granite counters and stainless steel appliances only to discover they can't command higher rents.

Multiply these costs by 25-75 units and you can see how the economies of scale actually work against you.

I know some investors who've done these high-end upgrades and, so far, they've managed to command very high rents for their market. They did it by promoting a brand that offers exclusivity and "pride of rentership."

Don't go with the single-family renovation guys.

While on the topic of unit renovations, here's a million dollar tip: Don't go with the single-family renovation guys. They will never understand how to renovate apartment units. In my experience, they will always want to renovate as if you are renting a house. I'll give you some examples in Chapter Six "Upside."

And lastly, the gurus will talk about...

Less Competition: The Market's Sweet Spot

The gurus love to tell you that as an apartment investor you will have very little competition from other investors.

They'll tell you you're in the elite 5% of investors—those who buy apartment buildings. But if you don't know how to source deals, you won't be investing in anything. Finding the deals that no one else knows about is a rare thing. The top brokers—those who have a ton of listings—typically pass those deals on to the property owners who have already bought deals from them.

The gurus will have you believe properties are available for a great price just because you asked. What they aren't telling you is this: one of the main reasons they hold real estate investing boot camps is so they can create a virtual pack of bird dogs who will beat the streets for hidden deals and gems. Those bird dogs are their students and through their sheer strength in numbers and manpower they find great deals. Often times they don't know what to do with the deal when they find it—so they bring it back to the guru for help.

We'll talk about some ways you can successfully source deals for yourself in Chapter Three "Acquisition Strategies."

Okay. I know you've got the idea. Commercial real estate has many advantages, but you really need to know what you're doing. And you have to be very cautious about buying into the hype.

It's not rocket science. But there are a lot of moving parts to investing in apartment buildings.

One of my real estate mentors told me something I'll never forget. He painted the picture by having me imagine a clock face. He told me that the time from noon to 2 p.m. represented what I know about investing in real estate. The time between 2 p.m. and 4 p.m. represented what I know I don't know about investing in real estate. And the time between 4 p.m. and 11:59 p.m.? That represented what I don't know I don't know.

Let's shed some light on those things you don't even know you don't know.

CHAPTER TWO

✳

"Buy real estate in areas where the path exists…and buy more real estate where there is no path, but you can create your own."
—David Waronker

Where Should You Buy?

Establishing Money Rules

You'll hear me talk about setting money rules throughout this book. In every business I've owned and in each investment I've made—whether in real estate, stocks, oil & gas, investment funds, start up businesses, or in other people's investment opportunities—I set certain investment criteria and I don't deviate. These rules are designed to keep me on track. I'll help you set your own rules as you read this book. (There's a form in the Appendix of this book where you can begin making your own list of money rules.)

Warning. The temptations to deviate can be great. Without firm money rules you can find yourself being tempted by every bright shiny object presented to you, whether or not it meets your investment criteria.

You'll end up doing deals you're not 100% sure about. You can find that your carefully laid out plans and strategies are in shatters.

> **It's easier to say "No" to opportunities that present themselves to you when they don't meet your criteria.**

You establish money rules to keep yourself on track. It's easier to say "No" to opportunities that present themselves to you when they don't meet your criteria. Do you remember the "10-unit apartment deal" I mentioned earlier? In my opinion, it wasn't really an apartment deal at all. It was a mish mash of detached units spread over 8 properties. When presented with the opportunity—and I'll add here that the guy presenting it was pretty enthusiastic about what a great deal it was—it was simple for me to say, "I'll pass on that deal. It doesn't meet my rules about economies of scale. I won't buy a property with eight roofs, eight heating systems, etc." He was cool with my response. In fact he was impressed that I followed a firm criteria for my investing strategies. Simple.

Here are some of my real estate investing money rules (you'll want to set some of your own, each person's set of rules will differ):

- **Everything is negotiable.** I know this seems pretty obvious, however if you don't ask, you won't get what you want. It's easy to ignore this rule. You might feel as though you'll insult someone if you ask them to negotiate. Or, you'll decide what the other person's response will be *before you even ask*. You'll never know what the other person is willing to do if you don't ask. They can't say yes if you don't ask.
- **Always make money on the front end of the deal.** I had

a 55-unit apartment building I was thinking about buying. A large hospital complex was relocating across the street from the property over the next couple of years. The broker and the seller worked hard to convince me this new medical campus (which hadn't broken ground yet) would positively impact property values throughout the entire neighborhood. However, the apartment complex in question was in a decidedly "C" neighborhood, meaning it was in a declining, less than desirable neighborhood. Property values were not increasing in this part of town. I couldn't see this neighborhood changing no matter what happened across the street. It was more or less like putting lipstick on a pig—and declaring the pig was now worth first prize in the state fair.

I made an offer on the property based on the current location and market. As I said, the neighborhood was extremely rundown. The demographic was questionable. The property was being managed by a landlord who paid very little attention to his residents. My offer on the property was rejected. Now, six years later, the medical complex is in place (and it's a beautiful campus, with multiple facilities) but the neighborhood across the street never changed. Property values did not increase more than 1% or 2%—for the entire six-year period.

The only way I would have done the deal was if I had negotiated a price that gave me a profit today. I won't bank on what *might* happen in the future. You shouldn't either.

Here's how negotiations might have worked:

» The seller was asking $3,000,000 ($3.0M) for the property.
» I offered $2,300,000 ($2.3M).
» I determined based on my analysis of the seller's financials that the property was worth about $2.7M —*after* repairs.
» Based on my analysis the property would require about $250,000 in renovations and repairs. This also took into consideration the fact that I would need to reposition the property in terms of the tenant base. In other words, bring in highly screened residents.
» If my offer of $2.3M had been accepted, I would have been happy with the negotiations.
» The seller, who was clearly struggling with the property, would have had a sale. The residents would have had a new owner who cared about their well being.
» After repairs my immediate upside was in the neighborhood of $150,000 ($2,700,000 estimated value – $250,000 repairs = $2,450,000. I paid $2,300,000.)
» Or, I could possibly turn around and list the property for $2.8M-$3.0M for an additional profit of $100,000-$300,000—after all, there *was* a big development moving into the area. Potential renters were relocating just across the street. There was a chance the new development would have a positive influence on the neighborhood and on the property.

• **Don't invest in an area you are not willing to travel to**. I see this happen all the time. You find a "hot" market. You acquire a property at a *great* price. You fly or drive to the property regularly over the first year. Pretty soon those trips become excruciatingly tiresome. The next thing you know three years have passed and you haven't visited your property once in the past two years. This is where trouble happens. As an owner of investment real estate, it is your job to stay on top of the manager, to visit and inspect your property regularly, to be the manager of your asset. When you stop visiting, you can lose control over everything. Why create an avoidable problem for yourself? When I buy a deal in a new location I want it to be fun to visit. My husband and I golf. So we might consider buying a property in a location where we can stay and play while we do a little bit of real estate work. We can also use at least a portion of the trip as a business expense. We love Mexico. We're currently involved in a real estate development in a part of Mexico we visit often. It is not a hardship to oversee our investment.

Money rules help you stick to your plan. Once you determine which types of properties you want to invest in—and the physical location of those properties—your search for deals becomes much easier.

List your criteria—*before* you start looking. If a property doesn't match—take a pass. Before you go look at it, before you picture yourself owning it. Don't even run the numbers on a deal if it falls out-

> **List your criteria—before you start looking.**

side any of your criteria (such as location). It's easy to become emotionally attached to the idea of ownership and to lose sight of how the property must perform in order to be a viable investment opportunity.

Remember, as you read this book, start making a list of your own money rules. Think back to Chapter One. Some of the rules you might have come up with from reading that chapter are:

- My property manager must be an owner operator of similar deals to mine. He/she has got to think like an owner.
- I won't do a deal without education and mentorship from successful multifamily investors.
- I'll think twice about what the real estate gurus are pitching.
- I'll learn about the potential pitfalls that might negatively affect a stable and predictable cash flow at my properties and I'll manage the manager accordingly.

Keep adding to your list of money rules as we cover them. Your personal rules might also include things like:

- The type of return you need to get to do a deal (ROI, or return on investment).
- The price range you want to buy in.
- Your holding period (including flips if you decide to go that route).
- Your exit strategies (will you hold, re-finance or sell?)
- How much of your net worth you'll invest.
- Whether or not you want partners.
- How much of your personal time you're willing to devote to your investing.

Your rules will be your own. No two people will have the same money rules. By the end of this book you will have a great start on your own set of investment criteria.

In this chapter we're going to discuss the importance of location.

Location Is Everything

Some "experienced" investors would argue that timing trumps location. I've heard the gurus say, "Forget about location, location, location. It's *all* about timing." In fact I heard a speaker recently say this at a real estate convention I attended. I sat in the room and watched the attendees take fast and furious notes. My impression? The speaker was trying to act as though he was smarter than the rest of the class. Was he just being clever debunking what most real estate investors believe? Or did his remark convince 55 convention attendees location was not a critical consideration when investing in real estate?

Timing in investing is important. However if you buy a property in a bad location, you've got yourself a bad investment. It doesn't really matter when you bought it. You might have a management nightmare. You may end up with a deal you could not sell to anyone but a rookie—and would you really do that to someone? I didn't think so.

Location holds the key when you're talking about real estate value. You can buy a cheap property in a dead market—and it's still a dead market. It doesn't matter how cheap the property was, you did not make a good investment.

Here's a story about Bob and Mike. They both decided to buy apartment buildings in Denver and were told "Central Denver" was the safest and most prudent area of town in which to buy apartment buildings.

Bob bought an apartment building west of York Street and Mike bought an apartment building east of York Street. Both properties were in Central Denver.

Over the next four years, Bob and Mike had vastly different ownership experiences. Bob, who bought west of York Street, had a property that performed very well. It was easy to rent. Property values increased.

Mike, who bought his property east of York Street, quickly discovered the top apartment management companies in the area wouldn't consider managing his property at any price. He quickly discovered there was a stigma attached to the part of town where his apartment building was located.

What Mike could have done differently was interview the local property management companies specializing in apartment building management before he bought his deal. Pretty simple right? It's a great idea to expand your network in any real estate market beyond the commercial brokers who work the market. Talk to property management companies. Talk to the vendors who provide services to the apartment industry. You can find out a lot about a market by getting out in the streets and by talking to people in the business.

You can find out a lot about a market by getting out in the streets and by talking to people in the business.

When I research a new market I have a list of vendors I contact. Here's a tip: contact the salespeople within those organizations—don't talk to the person who answers the phones. The salespeople are out in the streets dealing directly with owners. They see the properties. They know the neighborhoods. They're intimately familiar with different locations and demographics.

For instance, I call this list of companies:

- Trash companies that haul away garbage from apartment buildings.
- Laundry leasing service companies. Many apartment building owners lease their laundry room to service providers rather than owning their own laundry equipment.
- Landscaping companies. These are the companies that handle snow removal, lawn mowing, etc., for apartment complexes.
- Property management companies that deal only in apartment management.
- Neighborhood locksmiths.
- Lenders and banks that finance small, local apartment deals.
- Commercial transaction title companies.
- Apartment building engineers, appraisers and inspectors.
- Apartment building roofing companies.

I pick up the phone and network. Generally I just say, "I'm looking to buy an apartment building in your area. I'll be building a team of service providers and I'd like to know more about your service. By the way, what can you tell me about the market? Which part of town has buildings that perform really well? Which part of town would you personally avoid?"

If you stop your market research at the commercial property brokers, you've done yourself a great disservice. Talk to people who have a little bit less skin in the game e.g. they don't stand to earn big commissions on transactions.

And here's another really big tip, one of the best techniques I know of to source deals. The same people who interact every day with apartment buildings and their owners hear things. They know which properties are struggling. They hear of deals on the market, sometimes before the commercial brokers do. You'll read more about this in Chapter Three "Acquisition Strategies."

Speaking of Central Denver, it is a great market. It's the only Colorado market I'll consider investing in. The investors in my story really did get some good advice when it was suggested they invest in Central Denver but unfortunately for Mike, he didn't drill down far enough into submarkets. And you might say Bob got lucky. You can't look at a general area of town and say, "Okay great! I'll buy a deal in that market." Markets can literally vary street by street.

Most markets have submarkets. For example, in Denver you'll find Capital Hill, Congress Park, Cheeseman Park, Uptown, LoDo, Mayfair, Hale, City Park—all of these submarkets can be considered as being a part of Central Denver.

Last year I was looking at acquiring a 48-unit, two property apartment portfolio in the Capital Hill area with one of my investing partners. He was an experienced real estate investor but he'd never invested in the Denver market. One day we met with the listing broker to walk the two properties and to look around the surrounding neighborhoods.

This 48-unit portfolio consisted of two buildings. One building had 30 units and one building had17 units *plus* a little makeshift unit on the roof. This "18th" unit had been cobbled together (spit and glue) by the maintenance guy who worked at both properties. He lived in the unit. Guess how many units the property was marketed as having? You got it. It was listed as an 18-unit property. The unit wasn't to code and it was not city sanctioned, but the brokers were counting it anyway.

I'm getting carried away with my story, but I will never forget that little shenanigan. Misleading at best—or, an outright fib. I'll let you decide. Frequently, when shopping for apartment buildings, investors will use "price per door" as one of the criteria for determining value. In Central Denver the current average is about $73,000 per unit or door. By adding an extra (fictitious) unit, these brokers were attempting

> **By adding an extra (fictitious) unit, these brokers were attempting to bump the price significantly.**

to bump the price significantly. They also used the rent from this makeshift, not-to-code unit in their analysis of the financials even though a single property inspection could put that unit out of operation in a heartbeat.

The properties were listed as "turnkey", meaning very little needed to be done in terms of improvements or repairs. Fortunately we were able to visit the inside of some of the occupied units. To make a long story short, most of the tenants were in residence (this was at 10 a.m., in the middle of the week) and most were blithely unaware of our visit. They were passed out drunk or so high on drugs our presence barely registered. It was then I decided that if we actually bought these deals, we would need to take a fire hose to the properties. Clean them out, tenants and all.

Capital Hill has some great little neighborhood streets. This was not one of them. I'm familiar with single blocks that are not safe to walk at night—while others are showcase neighborhoods. We could have bought these properties, cleaned them up, and repaired a ton of deferred maintenance—only to own properties in a bad mini pocket of town.

Not all brokers are quite so misleading about their listings. This just happened to be one very questionable deal—especially at the current asking price. One last thing before I move on. As my partner and I stood on the roof, the one with the "penthouse", 18th unit, we saw a couple of guys looking up at us from the sidewalk below. They were wearing shiny suits and they had the dark sunglasses thing going on more or less like the blues brothers, or members of the mob. When we asked the listing broker, "Who are those guys?" he said, "oh them? They're my listing partners for these properties." The gang had arrived. Clearly they were thinking strength in numbers was required to convince their prospective buyers (us) that these properties were a great investment opportunity.

Questions You Should be Asking Your Broker

I know, or know of, most of the commercial real estate brokers in the areas I invest in. I work with only one or two—but I talk to all of them. Why? Because in general they stay on top of their markets and they pay attention to what other brokers are doing. They love to talk apartment investing. Commercial brokers can be a great source of local and national information. They love long, chatty phone calls. Ask a broker about a particular market and get ready for a 15-minute answer. Don't be afraid to pick up the phone and start networking.

Most commercial brokers will be happy to talk to you. You can get some great information during these calls.

In most cases, you'll be hearing a broker's personal opinion, but after talking to a dozen of them, you'll begin to get much value and you will find a broker you'll enjoy working with.

In the back of this book, you'll find a list of questions you can use when you talk to (or interview) commercial real estate brokers. The questions will help you get past the fluff—they will help you drill down to the stuff you really need to know.

Here are some questions I ask when I discuss real estate markets with brokers:

- "What markets do you work in? What can you tell me about them?" Be sure to drill down to submarkets.
- "What has the market been like over the past 10 years?" Here you're asking about property values, sellers vs. buyers markets, inventory and absorption (number of units built and their absorption into the rental market), Cap rates, rental rates, rental demand, vacancies, etc. Research historical data for all markets you are considering.
- "What is the apartment investing market like today? In your area?"
- "Would you tell me about the owners who've bought your listings?"
- "Of your clients, who has done really well with their investments? Why? What did they do to succeed?" Ask about their investment strategies. Find out when they bought those properties and when they sold. If they've

held the properties, find out how they're doing with them right now.

- "Do you have market research? Can I get a copy?"
- "Who else do you know with valuable market research?"

Researching a Rental Market

Craig's List (www.craigslist.org) and *Rent.com* (www.rent.com) will give you an idea for supply and demand for a particular area. You can research rental rates, volume of listings and competition for a particular submarket. Look for concessions such as free rent, free utilities, no deposits required, etc. If you find a lot of concessions they are having trouble filling vacancies.

Remember, when doing real estate market research it is critical to drill down to submarkets and neighborhoods.

Free Apartment Market Research Reports

There are some good resources online for free local apartment market data. Multifamily lenders such as *Red Capital Group* (www.redcapitalgroup.com) offer free research reports and commercial real estate valuation firms such as *Integra Realty Resources* (www.irr.com) also have free reports on local and national apartment markets. I suggest you visit their site and download the *IRR Viewpoint*, this is a great report that covers many national markets.

All of these reports may be free, but they are full of valuable information and well worth your time.

You'll also find free local and national apartment market reports at most large commercial real estate brokerages firms such as *Marcus & Millichap* (www.marcusmillichap.com), *Grubb & Ellis* (www.grubb-ellis.com), and *CB Richard Ellis* (www.cbre.com).

These reports include information on cap rates, vacancy rates, employment, construction & apartment unit inventory, housing & demographics, rents & capital markets and more.

Criteria for Locating Hot Real Estate Markets

The following items are the criteria I use when looking at real estate markets in general—including single-family and multifamily markets. A market does not need to meet every single item on this list to be considered as a potential area for investment. It should however include most. It's important to have a strong understanding as to how your target market stacks up against these criteria. In other words, you need to know your stuff—don't skimp on the research.

The top real estate markets should have:

1. Solid job growth and employment outlook – companies are hiring.
2. Growing employment base and jobs – the economy is improving.
3. Good population growth and density.
4. Strong rental demand.
5. High average market rents *or* rental rates on upward move (at low point).
6. Increasing leasing activity without tenant concessions.

7. Second or third-tier city with room for growth (population of one million or less).
8. Mild climate; located in Sunbelt.
9. High rating in national quality of life surveys. Growing in popularity. High levels of in-migration.
10. Median price of homes at 3-4 times median household income.
11. Income properties selling for 10 times annual rent or less.
12. Average vacancy rate of 7% or less.
13. Low crime rates.
14. Solvent financing in cities.
15. Lower tax rates than national average.
16. Location in the county seat.
17. Cultural activities, universities, and diverse economies.
18. Well established, long histories.
19. Low housing inventory.
20. Low housing foreclosure numbers.

In my advanced mentoring courses, we go into detail on each of these points.

A last word on market research. Don't stop after speaking with just one or two brokers. Read and understand every report you can get your hands on. Talk to the people who provide services to the local apartment industry. Talk to your mentor. Talk, if possible, to the other owners in the market you're considering.

Buying in the right market—at the right time—is critical to your success as a real estate investor.

CHAPTER THREE

✳

*Every person who invests in well-selected real estate in a growing
section of a prosperous community adopts the surest and safest method
of becoming independent, for real estate is the basis of wealth."*
—*Theodore Roosevelt*

Acquisition Strategies

It may seem to you after reading Chapters One and Two that my
partners and I look at some pretty seedy, dumpy properties. It's not
exactly true.

First let me tell you what we're not looking for. We do not
want to purchase turnkey properties. Those are properties
with very little deferred maintenance (i.e., there's no immediate need of repairs). They are at, or near, 100% occupancy and
the tenant base is stable (i.e., solid, highly screened, paying residents). These properties actually sound pretty good, don't they?

Which brings me to my point. The type of property you buy depends
on your individual investment strategy (remember your money rules).
A turnkey apartment building might be great for you if you want to

buy and hold a property long-term. The term "turnkey" basically means you buy the property, put the key in the lock, open the door and you're ready to go. It's also a good investment if you are leaning towards an income stream (assuming you pick it up for a good price) and a much more passive role.

In fact, if you're looking to hold a property long-term and your goals are to get a decent yield on your investment, a turnkey property may be perfect for your investment strategy. As you pay down your principle and build up your equity in this type of property you can expect to get good cash flow over the decades to come. It's also a great strategy if you do not have the team, the time or the financial wherewithal to oversee extensive repairs and renovations.

A turnkey property may be perfect for your investment strategy.

The reason my partners and I are not looking to buy turnkey properties (unless we should come across an extraordinary deal or price) is because we are bringing a Value Added Strategy (VAS) to our investment properties. We like properties with deferred maintenance and tenant issues. In some cases, the current owner has struggled with the property and is relieved to sell. It's easier to negotiate a great deal when an owner is stressed, burdened or overwhelmed by their property. In other words, they can be highly motivated sellers.

When we bring in our skilled renovation, leasing and management teams, we are able to quickly add value to the property (always assuming we purchased at a good price) and in doing so we can force the appreciation, or value, of the property rather than wait on market appreciation. We're also able to increase rents on the units—especially if the property has problem tenants. As we renovate and raise the look and appeal of the property, we can move out tenants and replace them with new residents at higher rental amounts.

Then we have the option of holding onto the property long-term or of selling it for a profit. I go into great detail on how to bring your own VAS to an apartment building investment in Chapter Six "Upside."

As I mentioned earlier it is critically important that you list your criteria before you begin looking for properties. How active do you want to be? This is a key decision and one you should make before you purchase a property. It's mandatory that you decide before you start looking at deals.

Would you like to buy something that is relatively easy to manage from the beginning—something that will require significantly less time on your part? Or do you want to jump into your investment as if it were a business, where you are leading teams of contractors, maintenance crews, managers, leasing agents, and so on?

Some would argue (especially the real estate gurus) that the only way to go is to force value on your investment by buying distressed properties and turning them around. I disagree. Both strategies (rehabbing/flipping a property or holding on to your property long-term) are viable options and you can do well in either case.

The Secrets the Real Estate Gurus Hope You Never Learn

When I decided to move from single-family real estate investing to multifamily investing it never occurred to me to attend a real estate investing boot camp. I've always invested in a mentor who worked with me one-on-one rather than attend a seminar with hundreds of participants where I become just one of many.

At the time, the apartment market in my area was pretty hot and I could have attended investing boot camps in my own back yard. The gurus were holding events all over town.

But I did have friends who were attending the seminars—often paying $5,000 to go to a single weekend event. They tried to talk me into coming along. It's kind of like strength in numbers. But I asked myself, "What if I took that $5,000 and worked one-on-one with a multifamily real estate mentor?" I wondered if I might have more success if I hired people who were already successful investors in apartment buildings and asked them to work directly with me. "Me" being the key word. After all, I had already realized significant success investing in single-family homes. What I needed was someone to help me work on my psychology around doing bigger deals—much bigger deals. There's a natural fear in moving from properties that cost hundreds of thousands of dollars into properties that cost millions.

> **You will be more successful if you hire people who are already successful investing in apartment buildings.**

The local commercial real estate brokers I interviewed suggested I start with 4-8 unit properties most likely because that's where I had prior investing experience. But I wanted to go bigger faster. At the same time I didn't want to make so many mistakes I'd lose everything.

Looking back on my decision, and talking to those friends who went to the real estate investing seminars, I made the right call. Why?

Because my mentors helped me build on what I was already good at doing. I had strengths in certain areas and my mentors helped me recognize and play on those strengths.

They helped me get out of my own way overcoming my fears including my fear that I would not be able to raise the funds to buy a multi-million dollar apartment building. My mentors also helped me learn to trust in my innate abilities—abilities like my solid negotiating and networking skills. There were definitely areas where I needed to become more educated and prepared in order to buy my first property. These were areas exclusive to me just as you'll bring your own fears, skills and talents to your real estate investing business. You know there's is no rule that states "Just because you're a beginner, you need

The real action and learning are out in the street.

to begin your real estate investing career by sitting in a seminar room with 500 other beginners and rookies." It's simply not true that you have to pay your dues in a classroom. *The real action and learning are out in the street.*

The best way to learn is to connect with successful investors. Ask questions. Listen to their stories. My mentors helped me discover strategies for acquiring deals. They connected me with people in my area who could help me find deals.

What about my friends who had attended the boot camps? They never did buy apartment buildings. They shared the common complaints I hear about all the time from my mentoring students who attended real estate investing boot camps before they hired me. They felt ill prepared to know if an apartment deal was a good one or not. They discovered no money down deals were elusive if not completely non-existent. They complained that the boot camps were low on education and high on opportunities to buy advanced mentoring courses. They simply did not feel as though they were ready to actually buy an apartment building.

Real estate investment gurus promise:

- Fast and easy money investing in apartment buildings.
- Anyone can do it.

I received an invitation to a seminar here in town just this week. Here's what it said:

"Create One Killer Cash Flow Deal That Can Set You Up For Life… you can buy apartments with little or no cash out of pocket. **How to Buy Without a Large Cash Down Payment!** Syndications are the name of the game in apartment investing!"

Do I even have to tell you how scary this advice is? This self-styled real estate investment guru is promising that you can buy a building with none of your own money by throwing a syndication together (a group of investors who will buy the deal for you!). Talk to a couple of real estate or syndication lawyers to find out just how dangerous this advice can be. And how costly putting together a proper (within the law) syndication can be. The risks include that you could run afoul of both state and federal criminal and civil securities laws pertaining to the regulation of investments.

I'm literally dumbfounded by these guys who put on weekend seminars. The promises they make are right of late night infomercials. In my opinion graduating students get:

- Enough knowledge to be dangerous. The students frequently don't know what they don't know (remember the clock face from Chapter One?). For example you can get in really hot water very fast if you put a syndication together in ignorance.
- Education just to the point of scaring themselves out of doing deals. In this case the students *do* realize just how much they still don't know.
- No idea that multifamily investing will not make you millions unless you treat it like a business.
- An opportunity to go out into the marketplace, source deals and bring the deals back to the gurus like good little bird dogs.
- A terrifyingly small amount of education about analyzing deals, conducting due diligence, negotiating and closing on deals. The gurus are counting on their students coming back to enroll in high priced programs.
- An opportunity to go to the back of the room and buy expensive products and programs.
- An offer to buy an advanced mentoring course for literally thousand and thousands of dollars. Graduating students of dubious success and training abilities often teach these courses.

Even with a no-risk money back guarantee (is there such a thing?), do you really want to go this direction with your investing career? But "Wait!" you might say. "These are great opportunities to meet other people who have the same interest!" I agree. You can meet many aspiring investors at weekend seminars. Yet most of the attendees are beginners. Wouldn't you rather network with experienced investors rather than rookies? Just a thought.

Oh and there's also the chance that you might want to become a passive investor in one of the real estate guru's deals, or possibly in one of the deals another student finds. But I'm guessing that the reason you are reading this book is because you want to be an active investor in one of your own deals.

The Truth Behind Mass Letter Campaigns

Okay, back to finding deals. In this chapter we're talking about acquiring properties right? Along with the different strategies for doing so. Here's a confession of how I wasted hundreds of hours taking some free advice out of a real estate training seminar my friends attended. After my friends graduated from the local real estate investing boot camp, they were really excited about an acquisition strategy they learned from the gurus teaching the seminar. It was contagious and I jumped on the bandwagon. I'll admit, at the time the strategy sounded pretty great to me too.

During the seminar the trainers recommended (and they still do) sending massive letter campaigns to all of the apartment building owners in a given target market. Letters saying you want to buy their building. Some of these letters are simply outrageous, saying things like, **"I just bought one property. Will yours be next?"** Unfortunately beginners are writing these letters. They've never purchased a property.

I spent hundreds of hours writing letters to apartment building owners asking if they were ready to sell their property. Why not? I figured the gurus had to know what they were talking about. I spent tons of time acquiring databases, even begging my real estate friends to give me their lists. I hired, trained and paid an assistant to print, stuff and lick thousands of letters.

And the funny part is, now that I own multifamily properties, I get these letters too. The students don't even write them in their own words. They just fire them off, trusting the deals will flow in.

It took me a while to realize that no deals were flowing in.

This was when I finally made a decision that there had to be a much less painful way to approach investing in this specialized real estate asset class. You can go straight to the source. You can develop relationships with real estate mentors. You can start hanging out with successful multifamily investors—people who have already learned by being in the trenches.

So how did I find my first apartment building? I made friends with apartment building owners. I hired a mentor specializing in investing in apartment buildings. My mentor suggested I start visiting with the property managers in my target market. I did—and that's how I found my first property. The deal did not come to me because I mailed out thousands of letters, and I found it in about 1/100th of the time.

Here are some great ways to start sourcing deals:

If you want to be successful you need to hook up with players already in the game. As they say in the PGA, "These guys are *good!*"

In Chapter Two we talked about all of the types of people who are connected to the apartment industry. These are the people you want to network with. Call them up. Take them to coffee. Ask them who they know. Attend their sponsored events. I have some friends in town that own dozens of apartment buildings. They also manage apartments and give free monthly educational seminars to the owners of the buildings they manage. These are the types of events you want to attend. You want to start rubbing elbows with the people who are active investors and managers.

Get active in Social Media. *LinkedIn* (www.linkedin.com) is a great place to join groups and keep in touch with people who share your interests. You will find real estate investing groups and groups that are specific to multifamily investing.

Do Motivated Sellers Exist?

They do. But they're not exactly crawling out of the woodwork. They can be hard to find. You can start by asking your connections if they know of owners who are having a really hard time with their property. An owner who has leasing, management and financial problems can be a very motivated seller.

Aside from your network you can:

- Drive around your target market and actually look for properties that need substantial work. I also look for properties that have cars in the parking lots during the day—this can mean unemployed and therefore non-paying or late-paying residents. Of course, it could also mean they have night jobs.
- Go on *Craigslist* or other rental advertising sites online and look for properties that offer excessive concessions

for the market like free rent, discounted deposits, free utilities, etc. If the other rental postings are not offering concessions, you may have an owner who is struggling to lease and/or manage a property.

- Look on those same sites for owners/managers who are posting frequently. You may see little or no advertising for other neighborhood properties, yet this owner has ads posting every day—even several posts in a single day.

I purchased a property from a group of relatives who had inherited two apartment buildings. I found the listing broker by networking with local property management companies. These properties were not listed publicly yet, in other words they were pocket listings of the broker. Networking pays off.

After inheriting the properties these owners held onto the apartment buildings for a number of years finally deciding to sell when the buildings had reached rock bottom. Because of incompetent property management, lack of supervision on their part and poor building maintenance they were finally forced to do something.

They had literally watched the properties drop in value over the several years they held onto to them. Who can blame them really? They didn't actively decide to be apartment building investors—they received them in an inheritance. I'm sure the family member who left them the properties probably had really nice apartment buildings at one point. But the new owners did not know what they were doing. We had to take care of significant deferred maintenance after we bought the properties.

Here's an important note. The relatives who inherited these buildings had no loyalties to the property. They didn't know the residents. They really did not care about upkeep. They were motivated to sell solely by the thought of hundreds of thousands of dollars at the closing table. They were purely motivated by cash.

By the time I came along and made an offer that my broker almost choked over because he thought it was too low, they were more than ready to sell. They knew they more or less had a monster on their hands. The property was getting worse by the day. Not only was my offer accepted, I was also able to negotiate a seller credit for some of the major repairs that needed to be done. We were able to replace the roof, sidewalks and driveways and put in a new courtyard all on the seller's dime. They even carried an off record second mortgage in the form of a promissory note! Now that's a motivated seller or sellers in this case.

One last thing my broker also almost choked on was the request for a seller credit for repairs too. But I insisted he take the offer to the sellers as I presented it. This is one for your money rules. You're still making a list, right? Your broker works for you—not the other way around.

This is one for your money rules.

You might be wondering what happened with the other property the relatives owned. We decided not to buy it primarily because of the bad neighborhood. We didn't see the potential for the neighborhood improving most likely for years and years. However, I do know the investors who bought it. By the time they did, the property was in such bad shape they couldn't get a lender to finance it so they bought the property for cash at a hugely discounted price. As I write this, they are in the process of completely renovating the property. And I guarantee they'll make a nice profit when they turn around and sell it. Cash deals can be a great way to go. If you are able to pay all cash (no financing) for a deal, you eliminate a lot of your competition for deals.

It's also a great idea to start meeting and networking with local apartment building owners. Many cities have apartment associations you can join. You'll have an opportunity to meet owners and service providers through these associations.

I know an apartment building investor who stayed in contact with the owner of an apartment building she wanted to acquire for years. The owner wasn't ready to sell but when he finally decided it was time he contacted her first and she bought it. Sometimes patience pays off. Even unmotivated sellers become motivated sellers at some point.

List Your Criteria Before You Start Your Search.

We've already talked about this but it bears repeating. List your criteria *before* you start looking to invest in an apartment building. If a property doesn't match—take a pass.

- Be clear about what part of town you want to invest in.
- Know how long you want to hold on to your investment property.
- Decide if you want to be an active or passive investor.
- Recognize that owning an apartment building can be like having a job. Do you want to do work on the property yourself or would you rather buy a turnkey property?
- Understand what type of property you want to own.

51

- Who will help you with your decisions? Will you hire a mentor? Network with other owners? Attend seminars?

The last thing you want to do is fall in love with a property that does not meet your criteria. Around my area we have some beautiful early 20th century buildings. The Art Deco style is magnificent. Every time I see one of these buildings I fall in love. But these buildings can come with a steep price tag—not only for the property itself (style and charm) but the cost of repairs, maintenance and upkeep can be sky high. This price tag I'm not willing to pay. It's easy to fall in love from afar and painful to discover the truth, especially if you buy an idea and it doesn't match your carefully laid out criteria. Once you own it, you own it.

Always remember that this is an investment. You may not live in the property yourself and it doesn't need to be a property that you would choose to live in personally. One of the things I love about renovating and repositioning properties is that I can create a wonderful living space for my residents, but it's not my home.

Apartment Building Styles and Unit Mix

Think very carefully about the type of property you want to own. They come in many styles and sizes.

In my area, you can buy several types of properties. We have walk-ups which resemble motels. These are properties with external stairways and can be one, two or three story properties.

We also have interior hall buildings. These properties have secure entryways and the units are entered through hallways within the property. I prefer the interior hallway apartment buildings. They are easier to market to potential residents because of the added layer of security and they can command higher rents. If you were a single girl living on your own which property would you rent? The one with your doorway on the street or the building that has a security buzzer at the front entrance?

What is the market sizzle? By this I mean, what are potential tenants looking for? In my area wood floors are a "must have." Is this something you'll need to add to a property in order to attract potential renters? We purchased a 1950s building that had beautiful oak flooring through-

What is the market sizzle?

out the entire property but it had been covered by carpet for decades. When we bought the property it was simple and inexpensive to remove the carpet and refinish the floors. When a potential resident asked, "Do you have wood floors?" and in this market this was typically the first question out of their mouths, we could say, "Of course. They're gorgeous. Come on over and take a look!"

Both of these property types can consist of various unit styles. Some properties only consist of studio apartments (sleeping area and galley kitchen all in the main living area—no bedrooms), some are one bedroom and some have two bedrooms. You'll also find buildings with a good mix of all three unit types. Typically the better the mix, the better the investment. Study your market and learn what types of properties are there. In my area the properties with all studio units tend to attract a more transient type of resident. For the right neighborhood, say a really high density, low income resident base, these properties can perform well. But you may be dealing with a higher turnover of rental units. The residents stay for shorter lease terms. Can your management company handle that demographic? Does it have experience renting this type of unit?

A mix of one and two bedroom units gives you an opportunity to market several types of units to several types of potential residents. A word of caution. Some markets will not handle two or three bedroom units well because the unit type is not in demand. You may have longer vacancies in those units and they may be difficult to lease.

Drive around your market and look at the different property types. Talk to the local management companies. Find out what type of units rent well—what type of unit and/or building is the market looking for? What is the sizzle potential residents are looking for? It could be something as simple as free Wi-Fi, which is an inexpensive benefit to offer to residents.

Networking is the Best Way to Find Great Deals

This is an bold statement I know. But here's the deal. If you're not networking you may never find a great deal. If you're not networking you won't know what the market wants. You need to start talking to everyone who is involved with apartment buildings, from managers, to owners, to the providers of service to the industry. Don't guess. Don't fall in love with a property because you would love to live there.

In the next chapter we're going to talk about some techniques to help you determine whether a property may be a good deal. One worth pursuing. Once you have your eyes on a deal these tips will help you decide what problems the property may present and will give you some great ideas for conducting your own due diligence. Before you buy.

CHAPTER FOUR

✳

*If you think it's expensive to hire a professional to do the job,
wait until you hire an amateur.*
—Red Adair

Be An Informed Investor

The single biggest mistake you can make as an apartment building investor is to buy a property and *then* discover the problems. This chapter will help you avoid making this mistake.

Knowing potential problems before closing on the deal will help you:

- Negotiate a better price.
- Negotiate a seller credit for repairs.
- Determine how much money you will need to have in reserves for operating the property.
- Determine how motivated the seller is.
- Develop a budget for renovations, repairs, maintenance, upgrades, and unit turns.

- Allow you to sleep at night. There's nothing worse than lying awake in bed wondering how you are going to resolve problems you never expected to encounter.

Now, stop reading.

Think about what you just read and go back and read it again.

In this chapter I'll be showing you how to investigate a property by driving by it *and* by visiting the property with your broker or with the seller. You will be able to use all of the information you gather on a property to:

- Negotiate a better deal.
- Figure out your cash needs beyond the purchase price, down payment, fees and closing costs.

What you read in this chapter and how you put it into practice, can determine whether you succeed as a multifamily investor—or fail.

Do you remember the apartment buildings I told you about earlier, the vintage, Art Deco style properties I love so much? This kind of property is a classic example of knowing what you are getting into before you get into it. If you'll recall, I told you they are gorgeous buildings but with a ton of needs. *Everything* is old: old plumbing, old electrical wiring, old plaster walls vs. drywall, old brick and mortar, old wood framing and old foundations. The list goes on and on.

When I talk to brokers in my target markets I always ask if they own apartment buildings. I ask about their experience as owners, what part of town they're in, how long they've owned. I ask just about any-thing I can think of. It was one of these brokers who steered me clear of these very old but very charming buildings. He owned one and he loved it, but he said he'd never buy another one again for the reasons I've already mentioned.

I was disappointed when I heard this. I had been driving around town and looking at apartment buildings, picturing myself as an owner, and frankly I had my sights on the very type of property he wished he hadn't bought. Oh well. It was a good thing to know. He may have saved me from a lot of grief down the road.

It pays to network. It also pays to get out in the streets of any market you are interested in and become very, very intimate with it. When I first decided to buy an apartment building I had the greatest fantasies of ownership. I absolutely loved driving around town looking at properties. I would suggest you do the same. Here's why:

It pays to network.

- You get familiar with your market.
- You help set the intention of ownership in your mind. Picturing yourself owning an apartment building is a great way to make it a reality.
- You learn to view properties like a pro. Like an experienced investor.

Brokers love to set property showings for their potential buyers. They want you to tour the property. It's sort of like cars salesman getting you into a new car and going for a test drive. They want you to picture yourself owning the car.

Today I won't visit a property until I've seen the financials. Why take time to visit buildings I wouldn't make offers on? But when you first start out you should go to property showings. Get to know the markets and the property types. Get to know the local brokers. See the residents where they live. Become familiar with the variety of property amenities available (more on amenities later in this chapter).

In this chapter I give you a list of things to look for on your visit. This list will help you view properties with a critical eye and I promise, most listing brokers will be impressed. You'll impress your friends too!

But first there's something I should tell you. When you physically look at properties be sure to exhibit the proper demeanor. Tamper your enthusiasm down just a bit. Look knowledgeable. Be cool. Ask questions but be really low key about it.

I'll never forget one of the first property showings I went to with my broker. I remember naively asking in a too loud voice, "How long has this property been on the market?" My broker looked stricken. The on-site manager who was showing us around became extremely agitated and fidgety. It was then my broker

I'll never forget one of the first property showings I went to with my broker.

whispered to me, "You don't ask questions like this when the residents can overhear you. Even if you think they can't overhear you. They have no idea this property is for sale. Tenants can really freak out if they know the owner is selling." Hey, we all make innocent mistakes, don't we? I'll guarantee you that I never did it again.

Over the years I've realized what great advice that was. Tenants don't want you to rock the boat. This is their home. When they hear the building will be sold they realize it means new owners and new management are taking over the property. It could mean changes for the worse and it upsets the status quo at the property. Even though you know you will do a better job for those tenants keep a low profile.

Okay, are you ready? Let's turn you into a professional prospective buyer. We'll start with what to look for when you drive by a property and then we'll go over a list of items you'll want to look for during a property showing.

Due Diligence: Before You Make An Offer

Here's some things to look for when you drive by a property:

- **Check out the cars.** Are the cars late model or are they run down, on blocks, parked on the lawn? If you are driving by during the day, how many cars are around? Ideally you want clients who are at their jobs, not hanging around their units watching TV all day.
- **Is there structural damage?** Look for cracks in the exterior walls and for any movement or shifting in the foundation.
- **Are the windows open?** In the winter? This could mean the property has heating issues. The boiler may be running too high. If the windows are open, and it's 30 degrees outside, the residents are too hot. If the owner is paying for the resident's heat this adds up really fast. In the summer? The same is true for air conditioning.
- **Is the trash overflowing?** Take a look at the dumpsters.

61

If they are surrounded by a huge overflow of trash the owner may not be scheduling enough regular pick-ups. As a buyer you'll know that the line item for trash on the seller's financials is too low. You'll need to adjust your analysis accordingly. While you're at it take a look at the type of trash that's lying around. It can speak volumes about the current residents.

- **Does the grass need to be cut?** This can be a good indication that the current management is not doing a good job for the owner.

- **Are the doors propped open?** If it's a secure entry building this is can be a bad sign. Why are the residents creating easy access to the building? It could mean a lot of traffic in and out of the building (drug traffic?) and a general lack of consideration for the rest of the residents. You want residents who treat a property like their home.

- **Are the windows old?** Will they need to be replaced?

- **Do the blinds match?** This might sound nit picky but a really good property should make a great first impression. If you have a mix of old, ugly, un-matching blinds, you are not presenting a good image. Maybe the current owner or manager doesn't care. If they don't care about something this simple what else don't they care about? By the way, you should match the blinds if you buy the property.

- **Is there a for rent sign?** How professional are the signs? Will you need new signage? Is there a "no vacancy" sign? This can be a good thing—the property is fully occupied. As a little side note here we never put a "no vacancy" sign at our properties. We'd rather encourage rental inquiries at all times and put a prospective resident on a waiting list rather than turn them away.

- **Do you see puddles of water?** If you see standing water on the driveways, sidewalks, roofs or, worse, along the building foundation, the property may have serious drainage issues. This is something you will need to repair quickly. If you decide to buy the property, you'll also need to find out how much damage has already been done. It may mean additional repairs are required.

- **If you can see the roof, how does it look?** Are repairs required?

- **Are there other structures on the property?** What type of condition are they in? Parking structures in particular may need: new roofing material, new line striping, new parking curbs, new security lighting, structural repairs, etc.

- **Is there trash on the grounds?** Shopping carts on the lawn? This will tell you what type of job the current management is doing. Tells you a little bit about the tenants and neighborhood too.

- **Are people loitering inside or outside?** What do they look like? Get a feel for who's hanging around the property.

- **Do you see shoes hanging from the high wires?** Urban myth has it this little trick is often used by drug dealers to notify their "clients" drugs can be obtained in the neighborhood.

- **Are brick repairs needed?** Does the property need to be painted?

- **Take a look at the asphalt and sidewalks.** Will repairs be necessary?

- **Look for electric meter units.** Sometimes the meters are inside the building but frequently they can be found along the property exterior. If the units are separately metered, the residents and not the owner are paying for electricity.

- **What does the building next-door or across the street look like?** You can tell a lot about the neighborhood by looking at the other properties on the block.
- **Look for things you can improve on.** For example, we purchased a property with a large loading only zone at the back of the building. We were able to block the area off, replace the asphalt with stamped concrete, add flower planters, picnic tables and a new tree. We turned the area into a beautiful courtyard. This became an excellent amenity for our residents and we used it in our marketing. It was very inexpensive to do. It definitely added to the "curb appeal."

Now let's talk about what to look for once you get inside the property.

Earlier I mentioned a group of investors in my city who do really high-end renovations on older apartment buildings. These are not new construction (Class A) apartment complexes. They take older properties, create a theme for each one and decorate the common areas accordingly. Their brand is phenomenal. Tenants love to brag about the fact that they live in one of these boutique-like apartment buildings. And the tenants pay a pretty steep rental price for the privilege. The units have upgrades everywhere you look. Granite countertops, stainless steel appliances, custom tile and wood flooring. Even the studio units are renovated to a super high quality.

One afternoon I was at my hairstylists' studio and we were talking about this book. She asked if I knew of these high-end (older) apartment buildings around town. I told her, "Yes, I know those investors pretty well. How do you know about them?"

It turns out a good friend of hers lives in one of these buildings. She told me she was really excited to go visit her friend for the first time because she'd been hearing so much about the building and about her friend's unit. But she was surprised at what she saw.

When she walked into the entryway of the building she saw signs posted everywhere. Signs warning the residents about mail thefts. There were warning notices telling residents not to have packages delivered unless they were present to take delivery personally. Packages were disappearing.

Her first impression was not a good one. In fact she told me she would never live in that building.

The reason I'm telling you this story is because you need to look around any property you are considering making an offer on. If possible go inside the building. Look around. You might see notices with information like, "The exterminators will be here on Thursday to treat for bed bugs. Please do not stay in your unit from the hours of 12 p.m. to 5 p.m." Or, "The water will be shut off to your unit from 8 a.m. – 4 p.m. for major line repairs." You never know what you'll see. Be sure to make note of things like this on your due diligence and negotiations checklists.

If possible go inside the building. Look around.

You may see something really cool like "We are having our resident appreciation barbeque Saturday afternoon. Please join us for free burgers and hot dogs." Managers frequently give information to their residents by posting notices in the common areas especially in the main entryway, mail area and laundry room. They'll also post notices on resident's doors. These notices can be a good clue to the building's personality.

As an owner I'm very particular about what my managers post in the common areas especially when we are actively leasing units. Good first impressions are critical to renting units.

Most showings are pretty short. You probably won't spend a lot of time inside or outside the property. Make the most of your visit. It's a good idea to memorize the following list or become very familiar with it at the very least. You don't want to walk the property trying to remember everything on the list. By all means take notes. But remember, you want to be cool during your visit. Act like you know what you're doing. Experienced buyers can walk a property and take in everything.

Here's why I say this. If you decide to make an offer on the property, *negotiations are not far off*. You want your broker and the seller to take your offer seriously. If you clearly know what you're doing they won't think that they've got an easy mark on their hands. Look like the pro you are. Take everything in with a casual eye and demeanor. You'll get better with practice.

You should have an opportunity to see inside some of the rental units, especially if there are vacant units. If there is a resident or on-site manager ask to see their unit. Don't take "No" for answer on this one. If the manager lives in the building, get in their unit.

Here's the list of things you'll want to make note of on your property tour:

- **Look at the lobby and mail area.** Are they clean? Read the posted signs.
- **Visit the laundry room.** Read the bulletin board. Find out if the owner of the property owns the washer/dryers and collects 100% of the revenue or if the owner uses a professional laundry service and splits the profits with the laundry leasing company—typically 50-50. Another thing to know and this is very important, most of these laundry leases run for 10 years and they stay with the property, not the owner. In other words, you will inherit the contract and the services of the laundry vendor. Ask about this on your tour.
- **Check out the boiler room.** Are there signs of rust, corrosion or scorching around heating unit? Find out how old the boiler is. Usually inspection notices are posted—look for them. Most boilers have a little plaque with information on the make and model. Check it out even if you don't know what you're looking for, make note of it. Over time you'll become familiar with the different brands and models. New boilers are an extremely high-ticket item.
- **Take a look at the roof if possible.** Many roofs have an interior access. Ask to actually get out on the roof and take a look around. Find out what type of material covers the roof. There are various types of material coverings, some more durable and longer lasting than others. Your broker should be an expert on this—ask. You'll also need to know if the entire roof may need to be replaced. Sometimes damage or age is significant enough that re-covering a roof is not sufficient. Remember the roof is the first line of defense protecting the property from the elements.

- **As I've already mentioned, get into the units if possible.** What kind of condition are the units in? Look carefully at the appliances, counters and cabinets. Check all ceilings and walls for signs of water damage. Do the doors fit well? A poorly fitting door can be a sign of foundation or structural problems. Warped or uneven floors can also indicate structural damage. If the property has a mix of unit types, see if you can quickly take a look at one of each type, even if the unit is currently occupied. Will the units need to be updated in order to command current market rents?

- **Be sure to walk all common areas including the back stairs and rear entryways.** Will you need to update the flooring (carpet, vinyl)? Do the common areas need to be painted? Are stair handrails in good working condition? Has the property passed fire inspections?

- **Look at the lighting fixtures.** Do they work? Do you see proper emergency exit signs? Will they need to be updated?

- **Look at the doors and hardware.** If the doors are hollow core you may want to replace all of them. Cheap doors can pose a security risk and good solid front doors on units can be used as a selling point to prospective residents. You may also need to replace the hardware, especially the door handles and locks for the same reason. Another consideration is that you may have to replace keys on all units or re-master everything.

- **Remember little things can add up quickly.** If you have 30, 50 or 100 units, replacing individual items can be extremely costly. Think of the cost of 100 doors, door numbers and door hardware. Or the cost of 50 new mailboxes. Keep this in mind as you evaluate a property. You are not buying a house; everything in a multifamily property comes in big numbers. Be sure you take note of these items.

- **Look for management signs on the resident units.** Things like eviction notices and warnings are a good thing to be aware of.
- **What does the property smell like?** Does the basement smell musty? There may be possible water issues. Are the residents burning incense? That's a great way to "disguise" the smell of pot or worse.
- **Are the common areas clean?**
- **What is the noise level?** Loud music, fighting, noisy parties affect all of the residents at a property.
- **Ask if the property has storage units for the residents.** Take a look. Find out how much they charge for renting the units. This is an area where you might be able to increase the income at the property.
- **While you're there take note of the residents themselves.**
- **Look for signs of bed bugs and mold.** Ask the seller and/or the broker if they've had past or current problems with this. If these items do not appear on the Seller's Property Disclosure I would add them to the document and make sure the seller signs off on both.
- **Ask about amenities.** Amenities can include such things as: free Wi-Fi, washer/dryer in unit, shared coin laundry, game, exercise, billiards, and cinema rooms, indoor or outdoor pool, in-unit security, controlled building access, covered parking, storage, internet lounge, coffee bar, professional landscaping, outdoor patio or courtyard, well-lit parking and sidewalks, and bike shed or racks.

As you can see you can leave a showing knowing a great deal about a property. The key is in knowing what to look for. You will surely ask questions during a showing but you can pick up a lot of additional information simply by being carefully observant.

While this list will serve you well for many years to come, please keep in mind that it is not all-inclusive. I cannot stress enough how important it is for you to have a mentor with experience in your corner.

And now I want to talk to you specifically about,

Bed Bugs, Pests, Addicts and Cops

This little header is a joke—sort of. I want to get your attention. Hopefully the properties you consider purchasing aren't this bad. But I'll tell you pests can be a problem. Even five star hotels, airlines and Class A apartment buildings can become infested with the dreaded bed bug.

You need to investigate whether or not this is or has ever been an issue at the property. A simple thing like a resident moving a "dumpster couch" into their unit can introduce pests to an *entire* property. It's a very expensive issue to address. Some full building treatments can cost upwards of $20,000 and come only with a 30-day guarantee. Are you prepared to do multiple treatments at that price? *And* it can cost you all of your residents. They move but the bugs stay. So not only should you know about infestation before you buy a property, it needs to be carefully monitored after you own the building.

You can search the property address online for bedbug reports at sites like *BedBugReports* (www.bedbugreports.com) and at *The Bedbug Registry* (www.bedbugregistry.com).

It's also not likely that your building will have addicts or drug dealers. But I think it's important to mention that a single bad resident can negatively influence an entire property. Undesirable "friends" of a bad tenant can start hanging around the property and good tenants will move out.

If it's offered in your area it's a great idea to get a copy of the police premise history during your due diligence. A premise history is simply a list of all police calls/visits to the property. It's very inexpensive to purchase. You can request a copy by calling the local police department. It includes everything: domestic fights, shots fired, 911 calls, medical emergencies, suicides and drug deals. Anything the police are called for makes the list. It's also a good idea to pull a premise history occasionally on the properties you own. Don't leave it to your managers to report everything. They may not want you to know what's going on and it's possible but not likely that your manager doesn't have a clear idea of police activity. A lot of this stuff happens at night.

Investigate Your Market

It's a good idea to investigate the neighborhood and the competing apartment buildings for a property you are interested in. What are your prospective competitors offering? What types of building amenities and upgrades do your competitors offer? Are most buildings renovated or dated? How does the location compare to other parts of town? Who lives in the neighborhood? What is the average demographic of renters? Average income? Where do they work?

You can contact apartment rental leasing agents and property management companies directly to gather this information. These companies are also a perfect source for getting information about market rents, concessions, vacancies and listing volume. Investigate your competition.

Due Diligence: After You Are In Contract

You will most likely present an offer to a seller via a commercial real estate broker in the form of a written contract. Most states have standard commercial contracts that are approved by the state real estate commission. I'd suggest you obtain a copy of your state's standard commercial real estate contract and read it. I'd also suggest you review the contract with your broker at the time of the offer if not before. Just make sure you read it and understand it. A mentor or lawyer can help you with this as well. The contracts contain performance deadlines you must be familiar with. Offers can also be made via a Letter of Intent (LOI). This is simply an offer in letterform that briefly outlines the terms you are willing to enter into. You'll find a sample LOI at www.theresabradleybanta.com/bookdownloads.

Once you are in contract you as the buyer have specific performance deadlines. Some of these deadlines apply to the timeframe in which you must complete your due diligence. These include the timeframe within which to respond to the Seller's Property Disclosure and the Buyer's Inspection Objection Deadline. In layman's terms the seller will disclose any latent defects known to them and the buyer has the right to inspect the property, at the buyer's expense, and determine if it is satisfactory or unsatisfactory.

Your contract should have a clause, sometimes called a "weasel clause", which allows you to get out of the contract if you object to anything that comes up during your inspection of the property. Be sure this is included in your contract. Typically the contract will state that the buyer can give notice to terminate the contract if their inspections uncover unsatisfactory conditions, at their sole subjective discretion. This can be something as simple as noise or odor. Clearly you want to do your inspections in good faith. You're not looking for reasons to get out of the contract. Discuss this with your broker or attorney.

Clearly you want to do your inspections in good faith.

You'll find a property due diligence checklist at the back of this book. This list includes all documents relating to the property. These are the seller provided documents you will be asking for as you conduct your due diligence on the property. You can download the list at www.theresabradleybanta.com/bookdownloads.

Here's the question that you need to ask yourself.

"How much money am I willing to spend on inspections—whether I close on the deal or not?"

Earlier I told you about the guys who inherited two apartment buildings. We bought one of the complexes. I also told you that we negotiated a seller credit for repairs (roof, sidewalks, asphalt, courtyard). This negotiating was done while we were in contract, in other words, an offer had been made and accepted. It's important for you to note that the negotiations continued after the purchase price was agreed upon. In this case, the sellers agreed to a $60,000 credit at closing.

While in contract I hired inspectors to inspect the entire property and to look at all of the property mechanicals such as the boiler, roof, plumbing, etc. I hired a structural engineer to do a full report on the property. I also hired someone to video the sewer line out to the street to be sure it was in good condition and free of breakage, tree roots, etc.

So the question is, are you willing to spend a little money to find out what you're buying or are you willing to take the seller and broker's word for it?

By conducting thorough inspections you'll know what you're buying and you can definitely use the information during negotiations. Personally I spend the money every time. I would never buy a property without completing full inspections.

One last thing, be careful about overestimating your own abilities. You may have some contracting experience or trade skills but if you haven't owned apartment buildings before leave it to the professionals. Don't do it yourself until you learn the ins and outs of apartment buildings and their mechanicals from someone who has prior experience working on these unique properties. For example if you've never repaired a boiler for a 30-unit apartment building don't start now. Red Adair said it well. "If you think it's expensive to hire a professional to do the job, wait until you hire an amateur."

Inspections are a critical element to your investigations. Be willing to spend a few bucks here. As I've mentioned several times the information you uncover through your inspection can be used during negotiations resulting in either a lower contract price or in a seller credit for needed repairs.

In the next chapter we'll cover how to get information from the seller and the listing broker in order to analyze the numbers on a deal. I'll also be covering an exercise I do with my mentoring students on how to ferret out the truth about what the seller and the listing broker are presenting in the Offering Memorandum.

CHAPTER FIVE

✳

Only when the tide goes out do you discover who's been swimming naked.
—Warren Buffett

Analyzing the Deal

There is an art to analyzing deals. And I'm not talking about the fancy spreadsheets you'll find the gurus giving away for "free." You know, you sign up for their course and you receive the one and only "$900 Cash Flow Pro Super Analyzer Software, while supplies last" —for free!

Do you recall the all-day apartment-investing seminar I mentioned earlier? The one where you could buy apartment buildings via syndication "with little or no money down!" Never mind that the law could come down on you like a ton of bricks for syndicating a deal illegally. My invitation to attend the event included the following, "Price of admission includes an easy to use software program to crunch the numbers to make sure you and your partners are getting tremendous returns on your money." Tremendous returns? Software will promise me that? I don't think so. Remember, garbage in, garbage out. Fancy software doesn't magically negate the need for good, solid, accurate numbers and investment assumptions like vacancy rates and market rents.

I don't care how fancy your spreadsheet is, if you don't know the numbers to put in it the spreadsheet is virtually worthless and a total waste of your time.

You can tell I get pretty adamant about this. Bad numbers are rampant. Sellers rarely list all expenses and frequently exaggerate income. Commercial brokers love to base their analysis on proformas—those are the numbers that might be true in a perfect world. One of my mentors loved to say, "If the grass looks greener, someone's been fertilizing." In other words they've been growing a new version of the truth.

Frequently, dare I say most always, the numbers presented in property offerings are generally coming from very creative imaginations. You'll never see them in reality.

So here's my first property analysis rule for you. When you are offered an opportunity to buy an apartment building, ask for:

- A current Rent Roll and
- The Seller's trailing financials (Annual Property Operating Data)

In this chapter I go into detail about both documents. But first let's talk about how you get the documents. You simply ask for them. You ask every single time you consider investing in a property. Even if

78

it's a deal in which you might partner with someone and take a less active role. Get these documents before you even consider spending time analyzing a deal. You may get some push back from the seller or the listing broker. Tell the offering party that it's your job to crunch numbers on any deal you are considering making an offer on and that you will not proceed without seeing actual property operating data provided by the seller.

In the literally hundreds of deals I've analyzed I've seen all types of property financials. Some are very complete with line items for all income and expenses. But you won't always get extensive, thorough, financials because the seller doesn't have them. Property owners are just like everyone else. Some are highly organized and others, well, you just have to wonder how they know anything about their property. Some property management companies are organized and have great accounting systems. And some seem like rookies. If you cannot get good accurate property records try for the tax returns. That's better than nothing.

> **Property owners are just like everyone else.**

If the seller has absolutely no financials or financials that are deplorably lacking in completeness it could actually be a good sign. It's clearly an indication of poor property management and of a seller who may be completely ignorant about their property. This may assist in your negotiations especially when you demonstrate that you know what you're talking about. Property owners may be unaware of negative issues at their property. A property may have rent collection issues. Minor and major repairs may be needed. Vacancies may be on the increase. In all likelihood the owner of a distressed asset will be more open to negotiating price and terms.

And need I say, there may be tremendous upside in the deal. When you buy the property based on it's actual financials you can negotiate a better price. Then as the new owner you can bring in a team that will be able to realize the property's potential. You can fix the deferred maintenance, bring in a new tenant base, command higher rents and you should be able to lower the operating expenses. This could be a great property for you to bring your Value Added Strategy (VAS) to. More on this in Chapter Six "Upside."

Ultimately it's you who must make a decision on whether or not to pursue a deal with incomplete financials. With time and practice you will become more and more familiar with certain property types in certain markets. If you're a beginner and all you can get is bare bones information from the seller you must be even more detailed in your due diligence on the property. Most properties will have a Rent Roll. It's a good place to start.

Rent Roll

The Rent Roll is a spreadsheet that lists the rental status of each individual unit in an apartment building. A good Rent Roll will include columns for:

- Unit Number
- Unit Type (one bedroom, two bedroom, etc.)
- Unit Square Footage
- Resident Name
- Lease Expiration Date
- Term: 6 month, 12 month, Month-to-Month (MTM)
- Move-in Date

- Vacate Date
- Security Deposit
- Starting Balance
- Rent (current and market)
- Additional Income (parking fees, storage fees, etc.)
- All Other Charges (late fees, utility reimbursement, etc.)
- Amount Paid
- Balance Due

That's what a good Rent Roll should include. Most don't. Most property management companies utilize accounting software specifically designed for multifamily and this software has the capability to include all of this information. I've had great managers with Rent Rolls that included all of the above. On the other hand, I had a manager on a property who owned full blown multifamily property management software but didn't know how to use it. With time and my insistence he figured it out.

I've also received "Rent Rolls" that looked as though they were written on a napkin. Sometimes that's all you'll get because that's how the owner does his/her books. Nevertheless, get what you can because a Rent Roll is a good snapshot of a property.

At a glance you will know:

- Number of vacancies.
- Future vacancies based on lease renewal dates.
- Collection history (outstanding balance due and late fees).
- Rent competitiveness (are rents at or below market?).

A current Rent Roll will show you exactly where the rental income is today. So for example let's say the listing broker or seller used the current Gross *Potential* Rent (GPR) in their financial analysis of the property. In other words this is the rent you receive if the property is at 100% occupancy. But what if *in reality* the property has a 31% vacancy rate? You'll know the numbers the broker used in the listing brochure are off because the broker is showing financials as if the property were fully rented. Do you see why you always want to get a current Rent Roll from the seller?

You do not want to base your sole analysis on *potential* numbers. It's good to know there is some potential upside in the financials—you will most likely be able to realize those *potential* rents the broker used in the future. However think about this. I can make two promises in this scenario. One, a bank will rarely loan on a deal with this vacancy rate. They will insist that you increase the occupancy before giving you a loan. Two, this is an indication of far greater problems. You'll want to investigate what's going on with those high vacancies. *Why* is the vacancy so high? What is going on at the property? A high vacancy rate should be a red flag to you.

Lastly, for the most part, you'll want to completely ignore the proforma rents on an offering brochure. If the current owner isn't getting those proforma rents chances are you won't either. One caveat: There's an outside chance the owner is collecting below market rents to keep happy, long-term residents. This can especially happen if the owner owns the property outright (has no debt service) and lower rents do not significantly impact cash flow. No mortgage payment equals higher cash flows. As a general rule of thumb however, do not use proforma rents in your analysis. You can view proformas as a potential upside but don't bank on it.

Later in this chapter we will be looking at an actual offering and you'll have an opportunity to compare the commercial broker's brochure to the seller's actual property operating data. I love challenging offering brochures. You will too!

Annual Property Operating Data

Annual Property Operating Data (APOD) are the documents that list all Year To Date (YTD) property expenses and income. These will usually be in the form of Cash Flow Statements, Balance Sheets, Profit and Loss Statements and General Ledgers. These annual statements will itemize all property income such as:

- Rent.
- Laundry.
- Parking fees.
- Storage fees.
- Late fees.

They will also include all YTD property expenses such as:

- Management fees.
- Taxes.
- Insurance.
- Repairs & maintenance.
- Utilities (gas, electric, water and sewer. Sometimes trash is included here).
- Advertising fees.
- Accounting & legal fees.
- Leasing fees.

- Make ready costs (the cost to make units rent ready after a vacancy).
- Landscaping.
- Common area cleaning.
- Trash removal.
- Pest control.

It's extremely important that you get copies of the seller's Annual Property Operating Data. This is important for several reasons. Two of the reasons are:

One, you always want to see the actual line item expenses on a property. When a broker or seller gives you an Offering Memorandum on a property listing they will rarely include all property expenses. Many line item expenses are lumped together. For example the category "Maintenance" might include repairs, renovations, supplies, the owner's telephone. You can never be sure. This is why you want the numbers from the seller—every time you look at a deal. For example if the pest control expenses are high in the seller's operating data it could be an indication of a pest problem at the property (bed bugs anyone?). But if that number is buried under "Maintenance" in the offering brochure you can miss it entirely.

Often times a careful review of the actual line item expenses can be very telling. Study each expense carefully. If you're new to investing go over a deal with your mentor or with an experienced multifamily property investor.

Two, you always want to see the actual annual income numbers from the seller. Frequently income will be grossly exaggerated in a listing brochure. It's important for you to review how the property has performed historically. In other words look at the numbers for the current date and for the past one or two years.

In the next part of this chapter I'm going to cover how to look at a broker's listing brochure and how to compare it to the numbers you actually get from the seller. While this won't cover every possibility, it will show you why it is so important to see how the property is actually performing today and in the recent past. You cannot rely solely on the offering information as presented by the broker or seller. Remember, they want the property to look great. They often use numbers (income and expenses) that support the asking price for the property.

Challenging the Listing Brochure

Have you ever wondered how much of a property listing brochure is accurate? Is the information verified and factual? Can you take the numbers to the bank?

I have a truly fun assignment I do with my mentoring students. We take an actual property-listing brochure slightly modified to protect the guilty and we find the many significant flaws in it. Let's give it a try.

And don't forget, you can find the exhibits used in this exercise as a free download over at my site, www.theresabradleybanta.com/bookdownloads. It will make it easier to follow as you read because you won't have to keep flipping back to the exhibits as I reference them.

Exhibit 1: Sample Offering Brochure Cover

Two Apartment Buildings: 45 Units!

Price Reduced!

Apartment Portfolio
PRICE REDUCED ~~$2,500,000~~ $2,375,000

Number of Units:	45
Total Square Feet:	24,684
Year Built:	1973
Price Per Unit:	$52,778
Price Per Square Foot:	$96.22
Proforma NOI:	$222,568
CAP Rate:	9.37%

INVESTMENT HIGHLIGHTS:

- Available Individually or as a Portfolio: 19 & 26 Unit!
- 45 One Bedroom Units
- Blocks From Medical Center & Hospital
- Significant Upside / Below Market Rents
- Walking Distance To Restaurants and Shops on South Main

Joe Broker
123 Main
Anytown, USA
555.555.5555

Let's see what you can tell by looking at the cover alone.

The price has been reduced by $125,000. As a property owner I never want to see this happen with one of my listings. "Priced reduced" just screams "Red Flag." Buyers may and probably should ask, "What's wrong with the deal?" At the very least you know the listing parties were overly aggressive with their initial asking price. In my experience in analyzing hundreds of deals, the price is still probably very aggressive even at the lower price. Large egos may be at play here. You'll see what I mean by this when we get to the financials.

When a listing brochure has *nothing* to say about the property itself, and everything to say about its great location, you can be sure the property has significant deferred maintenance. The cover of the brochure highlights: "Walking Distance to Restaurants and Shops" and "Blocks from Medical Center & Hospital." So now you need to ask yourself, "Just how much deferred maintenance is there???" You have my word on it, if one single renovation had been completed at the property most likely in the past 5-10 years the broker/seller would be touting it to the skies.

For example you'd see copy such as "All new windows" and "Most units have been recently updated!" or "Almost new boiler" and "Newer roof." When a property brochure has no glowing reports about the property itself and has only great things to say about the neighborhood, it's safe for you to assume the property has seen little in terms of recent renovations and updates.

These two items are the biggest red flags I see when looking at this cover.

But there's more. The property highlights also include "Significant Upside and Below Market Rents!"

"Wow!" you say. "I can raise the rents! I should be able to rent this property all day long to the employees of those huge hospitals! Think of the cash flow! Think of the increased property value when I up those rents!"

And that's exactly what the broker/seller wants you to think. As an aside here—if it were that easy to raise the rents, it would have been done already. There are very few exceptions.

So, what's missing here?

Again, there's absolutely nothing written about the property itself. The property description simply states the apartment complex is a "Portfolio of buildings (one 19-unit building and one 26-unit building) consisting of 45 One Bedroom Units" which as I pointed out in Chapter Three is a pretty poor unit mix. I like to buy properties with a unit mix of at least one and two bedroom units. Especially if there is market demand for both types. It broadens your marketing ability and offers choices to prospective residents. Get to know your market. You may find there is little demand in your location for only one bedroom units.

Ready to buy? Not so fast. After a careful analysis of this offering and taking a good look at the seller provided annual financials you'll see the asking price of $2,375,000 is considerably too high.

And now we get back to my first property analysis rule: Get the actual numbers from the seller. Ask for them!

Take a look at Exhibit 2: Sample Offering Brochure Financials

| Unit Mix & Rent Schedule | | | | | | Current | |
No. Units	Type	SF	Current Rent		Market Rent		Current Rent/SF
9	1Bd/1Ba	565	$	550	$	600	$ 0.97
10	1Bd/1Ba	530	$	510	$	550	$ 0.96
9	1Bd/1Ba	565	$	550	$	600	$ 0.97
17	1Bd/1Ba	540	$	510	$	550	$ 0.94
	Averages		$	536.67	$	583.33	$ 0.97
45	Totals	24,650	$23,670.00		$ 25,650.00		

Income	Current	Proforma
Rent Income	$ 284,040	$ 307,800
Less Vacancy & Credit Loss	$ (14,202)	$ (15,390)
Plus Other Income	$ 5,488	$ 37,898
Effective Gross Income	$ 275,326	$ 330,308

Expenses	Estimated	Proforma
Taxes	$ 10,736	$ 10,736
Insurance	$ 7,875	$ 7,875
Maintenance/Repairs	$ 20,250	$ 20,250
Management	$ 15,124	$ 15,124
Utilities	$ 37,542	$ 37,542
Miscellaneous	$ 16,213	$ 16,213
Total expenses	$ 107,740	$ 107,740
Per Unit	$ 2,394	$ 2,394
Per Square Foot	$ 4.37	$ 4.37
Net Operating Income	$ 167,586	$ 222,568
Less: Annual Debt Service	$ (131,610)	$ (131,610)
Cash Flow	$ 35,976	$ 90,958
Cash-on-Cash	6.06%	15.32%
Principal Reduction	$ 20,873	$ 20,873
Total Return	9.57%	18.83%
Cap Rate	7.06%	9.37%

You'll see the "current" Net Operating Income (NOI) for the properties is $167,586. The NOI is simply the total property income minus the total operating expenses. Mortgage payments are not included in NOI.

Here's how they arrived at the numbers:

$275,326 (income) - $107,740 (expenses) = $167,586 (NOI)

Now take a look at the proforma NOI. It's a cool $222,568. This is $54,000 and change higher than the "current" NOI. It's almost 25% higher!

Again, here's how they arrived at the numbers:

$330,308 (income) - $107,740 (expenses) = $222,568 (NOI)

You can see that the expenses of $107,740 remain the same in both scenarios. First of all, I have to say that's extremely odd in itself. Most proforma financials will show an improvement in expenses. In other words, the broker/seller will lower the annual expenses in their proforma financials. They will claim that by simply managing a property better and more efficiently you as the new owner will be able to lower expenses across the board. And often that's true. It's just unusual that they didn't do it here.

Perhaps it's because they want the prospective buyer to focus solely on the potential "upside" to income. Clearly they want to the buyer to believe they can increase the property income by almost 25%! That's a huge increase. If the income could have been raised this dramatically the current owner would have done it.

So the first question I would ask myself is this, "If this property has a ton of deferred maintenance, as I suspect it does, how can I ever expect to command market rents?" An un-renovated property, in dire need of improvements, will have steep competition from other properties without deferred maintenance.

Now, let's take a look at the seller's annual operating data from the previous year—January thru December. These numbers are not in the Broker's Offering Memorandum. I asked the seller via the listing broker to provide this information. Do you remember my first property analysis rule? You must ask for the seller's trailing financials. I can't think of a better example than the example below, of why this rule is so important to your due diligence. You'll see the seller's numbers in Exhibit 3.

Exhibit 3: Seller Provided Financials

Seller Provided Financials					
Annual Income	Bldg 1		Bldg 2		Totals
Prepay Income (?)	$	(1,619.29)	$	984.96	$ (634.33)
Monthly Rent	$	84,275.12	$	126,236.68	$ 210,511.80
Garage/Parking			$	(25.00)	$ (25.00)
Other Income/Refunds	$	495.00	$	(354.00)	$ 141.00
Legal Fee Income	$	360.00	$	360.00	$ 720.00
Tenant Reimbursement	$	1,201.55	$	565.06	$ 1,766.61
Interest			$	9.37	$ 9.37
Laundry & Vending Income	$	1,856.05	$	3,077.16	$ 4,933.21
Late Fees/NSF Ck Income	$	(5.00)	$	(360.90)	$ (365.90)
Total Income Collected	$	86,563.43	$	130,493.33	**$ 217,056.76**
Annual Op Expense - EOY 2008	Bldg 1		Bldg 2		Totals
Advertising PR	$	1,109.60	$	48.00	$ 1,157.60
Appliances - New	$	1,017.34	$	1,156.97	$ 2,174.31
Appliances - Used	$	-	$	433.22	$ 433.22
Bank Charges	$	90.00	$	281.25	$ 371.25
Cleaning Vacant Unit	$	1,269.00	$	944.50	$ 2,213.50
Carpet Cleaning	$	623.00	$	930.00	$ 1,553.00
Carpet New	$	1,580.42	$	-	$ 1,580.42
Cleaning Supplies	$	-	$	124.50	$ 124.50
Drain Cleaning	$	147.00	$	95.00	$ 242.00
Boiler/Elevator	$	24.50	$	-	$ 24.50
Physical Eviction Cost	$	161.50	$	197.00	$ 358.50
Fire Protection	$	34.16	$	-	$ 34.16
Ins - Fire & Extend Cov	$	1,488.20	$	5,740.50	$ 7,228.70
Leasing Fees	$	225.00	$	150.00	$ 375.00
Legal	$	1,031.00	$	1,000.00	$ 2,031.00
Licenses, Fee, Permits	$	-	$	50.00	$ 50.00
Lock service	$	322.00	$	319.50	$ 641.50
Maintenance	$	385.50	$	844.00	$ 1,229.50
Maintenance Supplies	$	3,908.37	$	8,987.35	$ 12,895.72
Make Ready Maintenance	$	4,441.50	$	2,064.50	$ 6,506.00
Management Fees	$	4,857.03	$	7,442.13	$ 12,299.16
Misc Expense	$	29.89	$	-	$ 29.89
Painting Labor	$	875.00	$	1,750.00	$ 2,625.00
Pest Control	$	1,377.00	$	1,822.00	$ 3,199.00
Parking Lot	$	-	$	1,569.02	$ 1,569.02
Resident Manager	$	1,968.49	$	1,900.00	$ 3,868.49
Payroll Tax Escrow	$	256.90	$	325.41	$ 582.31
Repair - Appliance	$	164.00	$	293.50	$ 457.50
Repair - Electrical	$	265.50	$	68.50	$ 334.00
Repair - Plumbing	$	2,454.50	$	2,329.00	$ 4,783.50
Repair - General	$	1,135.00	$	561.50	$ 1,696.50
Repair - Dry Wall	$	36.50	$	300.00	$ 336.50
Repair - Heating	$	522.88	$	1,038.00	$ 1,560.88

Exhibit 3: Seller Provided Financials (cont.)

Screens	$ 46.50	$ -	$	46.50
Sewer/Wastwater	$ 46.50	$ 24.50	$	71.00
Snow Removal	$ 172.75	$ 280.63	$	453.38
Tax - Pers Prop	$ 4,822.86	$ 84.05	$	**11,115.44**
UNPAID TAX (LIEN)		$ 6,208.53		
Telephone	$ -	$ 480.00	$	480.00
Trash Removal	$ 3,569.60	$ 4,229.61	$	7,799.21
Travel	$ 35.50	$ -	$	35.50
Utilities - apartments	$ 2,840.39	$ 6,517.31	$	9,357.70
Utilities	$ 9,615.38	$ 11,707.95	$	21,323.33
Water	$ 3,381.20	$ 5,240.06	$	8,621.26
Window Replacement	$ 242.44	$ 84.95	$	327.39
Window Coverings	$ 68.50	$ 35.50	$	104.00
Yard Care	$ -	$ 343.00	$	343.00
Total Annual Expenses	$ 56,642.40	$ 78,001.44	**$ 134,643.84**
Net Operating Income	$ 29,921.03	$ 52,491.89	**$ 82,412.92**
Debt Service			$ 92,619.00
NOI After Debt Service			**$ (10,206.08)**
Capital Expenses	$ 327,000.00		
NOI after Debt and Capital			
Cumulative Cash Needs			

Loan: $1.19M at 6.75% ($1.7M, 70% LTV)

If you'll recall, the brokers listed the "estimated" Net Operating Income (NOI) in their Offering Memorandum at $167,586. Usually a brochure will list NOI as "current" not "estimated" but in this case I guess the brokers were more or less covering their you-know-what's. They must have figured it was safer to say "estimated" than "current." Watch the language used in a brochure carefully.

When you look at the seller provided financials you will see the actual NOI on the two properties for the previous year was $82,412.92.

That's it—$82,412—*less than half of the "estimated" NOI* as listed in the offering brochure.

Here's how you arrive at the numbers:

$217,056 (income) - $134,643 (expenses) = $82,413 (NOI)

So who's to be believed? And don't forget the brokers also listed the proforma NOI at an unbelievable $222,568. To summarize, last year the seller had a NOI of $82,412, the brokers are "estimating" current NOI to be $167,584 and they want you to believe you can buy the property and realize a NOI of $222,568.

Now are you beginning to see why I think the asking price is over inflated? Clearly some due diligence is in order. So "What's wrong here?" you might ask. Good question.

Let's take a look at the current Rent Roll in Exhibit 4.

Exhibit 4: Seller Provided Rent Roll

Rent Roll - Current						
	Bldg 1		Bldg 2		Totals	
Unit	Rent		Rent		Rent	
101	$	495.00		Manager	$	495.00
102	$	475.00	$	510.00	$	985.00
103	$	550.00	$	550.00	$	1,100.00
104	$	495.00	$	495.00	$	990.00
105	$	475.00	$	520.00	$	995.00
106		n/a*	$	495.00	$	495.00
107		n/a	$	475.00	$	475.00
108		n/a	$	460.00	$	460.00
201	$	495.00	$	495.00	$	990.00
202	$	495.00		VACANT	$	495.00
203		VACANT		VACANT	$	-
204	$	475.00	$	495.00	$	970.00
205	$	450.00	$	450.00	$	900.00
206		VACANT	$	495.00	$	495.00
207	$	500.00	$	495.00	$	995.00
208		n/a		VACANT	$	-
301	$	515.00	$	450.00	$	965.00
302		VACANT		VACANT	$	-
303		VACANT	$	475.00	$	475.00
304		VACANT	$	495.00	$	495.00
305	$	495.00	$	450.00	$	945.00
306	$	495.00	$	450.00	$	945.00
307	$	450.00		n/a	$	450.00
308		n/a	$	510.00	$	510.00
309		n/a		VACANT	$	-
Total	$	6,860.00	$	8,765.00	$	15,625.00
Vacancy		27%		21%		

*Building does not have units mark as "n/a"

Remember this is the current Rent Roll, a document I obtained from the seller. This is a snapshot of the property today. Here's what I see.

- The properties are at an occupancy rate of 73% and 79%.

In other words a vacancy rate of 27% and 21%.

- The offering brochure stated that there were a total of 45 units between the two properties. The Rent Roll shows only 19 units in one building and 24 in the other. By my accounting those numbers total 43 units. We're missing two whole units.

- Take a good look at the Unit Mix & Rent Schedule in the Sample Offering Brochure (Exhibit 2) and compare the "current rent" to the actual Rent Roll the seller provided (Exhibit 4). The brokers have listed the current rent at $510 to $550, yet you'll notice from the seller's Rent Roll that very few units actually rent for an amount above $500. Most units are renting between $450 and $495.

- Now look at the "market rent" in the Sample Offering Brochure. The brokers are suggesting here that the new owner can rent units for $550 to $600 per unit. I know, because I'm familiar with this market, that the broker's "market rent" of $600/unit in the offering brochure is fiction. One bedroom units in this market do not rent for more than $550, even units that have been nicely renovated. Even properties with high-end amenities are not getting $600/unit. Do your homework and be clear on market rents in your particular location.

Now let's take a look at the income if the property were fully rented (Exhibit 5 below).

Exhibit 5: Seller Provided Rent Roll Assuming Full Occupancy

Rent Roll - Fully Rented						
	Bldg 1		Bldg 2		Totals	
Unit	Rent		Rent		Rent	
101	$	495.00		mgr	$	495.00
102	$	475.00	$	510.00	$	985.00
103	$	550.00	$	550.00	$	1,100.00
104	$	495.00	$	495.00	$	990.00
105	$	475.00	$	520.00	$	995.00
106		n/a*	$	495.00	$	495.00
107		n/a	$	475.00	$	475.00
108		n/a	$	460.00	$	460.00
201	$	495.00	$	495.00	$	990.00
202	$	495.00	$	425.00	$	920.00
203	$	425.00	$	425.00	$	850.00
204	$	475.00	$	495.00	$	970.00
205	$	450.00	$	450.00	$	900.00
206	$	495.00	$	495.00	$	990.00
207	$	500.00	$	495.00	$	995.00
208		n/a	$	425.00	$	425.00
301	$	515.00	$	450.00	$	965.00
302	$	495.00	$	425.00	$	920.00
303	$	495.00	$	475.00	$	970.00
304	$	450.00	$	495.00	$	945.00
305	$	495.00	$	450.00	$	945.00
306	$	495.00	$	450.00	$	945.00
307	$	450.00		n/a	$	450.00
308		n/a	$	510.00	$	510.00
309		n/a	$	495.00	$	495.00
Total	$	9,220.00	$	10,960.00	$	20,180.00
Vacancy		0%		0%		
*Building does not have units mark as "n/a"						

At full occupancy, the listing brochure puts the current annual "Rent Income" at $284,040. The actual number in the Rent Roll (Exhibit 5) at full occupancy is $242,160 (monthly rent of $20,180 x 12). That's **$41,800** less than what the broker used in the income statement on the listing brochure. Don't forget, these numbers are used to arrive at the asking price. It's a huge difference. This is why I suggest you get the real numbers from the seller.

There are a couple of other things I want to point out about this "deal."

After reviewing the brochure and the seller provided financials I spoke with the listing broker to ask about the current condition of the property. Remember the brochure praised the location of the property but said nothing about deferred maintenance. My further inspections of the property uncovered the fact that the property had significant deferred maintenance as follows (Exhibit 6):

Exhibit 6: Estimated Capital Expenses

Estimated Capital Expenses			
Full Unit Renovate $2800/u	$ 126,000.00		
Roofs	$ 50,000.00		
Boilers	$ 24,000.00		
Walk-up Stairs	$ 15,000.00		
Asphalt	$ 40,000.00		
Plumbing	$ 20,000.00		
General Repairs	$ 30,000.00		
Common Areas	$ 12,000.00		
Air Conditioning Units	$ 10,000.00		
Total Capital Expenses	$ 327,000.00		

Now we know why the listing broker didn't include recent property improvements in the "Property Highlights." There were none. Ultimately this property will need a lot of TLC and repairs in order to command the income as presented in the offering brochure.

When I made an offer on this property I based the offer on my revised NOI, one that represented current reality. I also factored in the total capital expenses needed to bring the property to rentable condition. Would you like to know what offer I made? And how I did it? Go download the Letter of Intent (LOI) and the Sample Comprehensive Proposal document from my site at www.theresabradleybanta.com/bookdownloads. This free document is the actual letter I gave to the seller of the properties and goes into tremendous detail about how I arrived at a potential purchase price. This is a great reference for you to use when you receive a ridiculously high counter offer from a seller. It's also a wonderful document to use if you want to put a thorough and well-researched offer in front of a potential seller who may have vastly overinflated ideas as to the value of their property.

In the end, I didn't pursue this property. The seller would not drop the asking price to the point where I would actually have interest in the deal.

One other thing of note, you'll see a line item on the seller's annual operating data called "UNPAID TAX (LIEN)" in the amount of $6,208.53. The seller or the listing broker did not disclose this fact. It appears as a line item because I included it for the purpose of the exercise. When I went online to verify the property tax amounts I discovered a tax lien on the property. This expense was included in the seller's numbers as *paid*.

I could talk about challenging statements in a listing broker's brochure all day but could never fit it into a single chapter in a book. This particular deal was a classic. The omissions and errors in the example above were numerous. I continue to use it as a training tool today. In all, there are around 20 misstatements in this one listing. Too much to cover here. Let me know if you like this sort of thing. I'd be happy to review it with you.

I strongly suggest you start looking at deals in your market of choice. Compare at least 10 similar offerings side by side. Include seller's numbers in your analysis. Start looking at rents and expenses, especially line item expenses, for similar deals. Refer to Exhibit 3 as a good example of the types of expenses you will have as an owner of a multifamily property. This level of detail does not appear in a listing brochure. It's your job to know all of the expenses you will incur as a property owner.

With time and practice you'll begin to get a feel for what the numbers should look like. You'll also get some great experience in ferreting out truth from fiction in listing brochures.

CHAPTER SIX

✳

If I had eight hours to chop down a tree,
I'd spend six sharpening my axe.
—Abraham Lincoln

Upside

I like to buy apartment buildings in need of improvements but usually not in need of major renovations. Poor management and distracted property owners often lead to deferred maintenance. Simple cosmetic fixes can dramatically force property appreciation by raising income and lowering expenses. For example installing energy efficient lighting in the common areas is a very inexpensive way to lower costs. You can improve curb appeal by planting shrubs and flowers and attract new renters to your property. You can clean and paint the common areas such as entryways, hallways, and storage and laundry rooms.

These are simple and inexpensive things to do.

When you raise the Net Operating Income (NOI) on a multifamily property you also raise the value on the property.

As you saw in the previous chapter, NOI is simply your property income less your property expenses before debt service. In the example below, if you have a NOI of $100,000, at a cap rate of 8% your market value equals $1,250,000.

$$\$100,000 / .08 = \$1,250,000$$

If the cap rate stays the same and you raise your NOI by $20,000 you will increase the market value of your property by $250,000 as shown below:

$$\$120,000 / .08 = \$1,500,000$$

What's a Cap Rate?

Here's a short primer on cap rates. A capitalization (cap) rate is simply your assumed, unleveraged rate of return (cash) before mortgage payments and income taxes. Let's take a look at three quick formulas. The first one you already know from the example above.

NOI divided by Cap Rate = Market Value
($120,000 / .08 = $1,500,000)

NOI divided by Market Value = Cap Rate
($120,000 / $1,500,000 = .08)

Market Value times Cap Rate = NOI
($1,500,000 x .08 = $120,000)

When you know two of the three factors, Cap Rate, Market Value, and/ or NOI, you can arrive at the third. When *buying* a property a higher cap rate is better. Using the same math from our property above a NOI of $120,000 at an 8% cap equals a market value of $1,500,000:

$$\$120,000 \,/\, .08 = \$1,500,000$$

But at a higher cap rate, say 10%, the market value decreases by $300,000:

$$\$120,000 \,/\, .10 = \$1,200,000$$

As you can see from the next example when *selling* a property, a lower cap rate is better. In this example, the market value is two million dollars at a 6% cap rate:

$$\$120,000 \,/\, .06 = \$2,000,000$$

Remember cap rates are not the only criteria to use when evaluating a deal. Cap rates are the most commonly used criteria for screening commercial investment properties but they are not perfect. Don't find yourself valuing a property on the cap rates your broker or seller uses. Remember most investment summaries are based on proforma numbers and they are based on frequently inaccurate NOI. Again, do your homework.

I guarantee you that when you own a property you will watch your market cap rates closely. If for example you bought your property at a cap rate of 6% and the market realizes upward pressure on caps (i.e., they start to rise), you will take notice. You can see your property value drop before your very eyes as shown by the math above.

This is another reason why one of my real estate investing money rules for any type of real estate is, "Always make money on the front end of the deal." Unless you plan to hold your real estate acquisitions for the very long-term and you are not relying on your investment to bail you out financially if you encounter bad times, you must buy at a price that makes you a profit today. In other words, you've got to find good deals.

Value Added Strategies

Before I go on here's another caveat about creating upside in your investment with value added strategies (VAS). The gurus and most of the popular books I've read on investing in apartment buildings will tell you this is the only investment strategy to follow. They suggest you buy properties with significant but not major deferred maintenance. They'll tell you to look for properties that are poorly managed and are filled with undesirable tenants. The idea is to ride in on a white horse wearing your white hat and save the day. You buy the property "for a great price" because it's in a downward spiral. You fix up the cosmetics, run the residents out or improve tenant relations and raise the rents. Then you can sell the deal for a fantastic profit a.k.a. force appreciation.

> **You need to have a team that knows what they're doing.**

The danger here is that you may not know what you're doing. Or you may not have enough time to manage the process. Or you may have the wrong team. Or you may decide you don't want to invest in a property that needs this amount of work. You may want a turnkey property in need of very little work.

What the gurus frequently fail to warn you about is:

- You need to have a team that knows what they're doing.
- More importantly you need to know what you're doing in order to lead your team.
- You need to be properly funded.
- You need to buy the property at the right price.
- You must have reserve funds.
- You need a solid plan and a plan for contingencies.
- You must have the time to oversee the project. In many ways repositioning a property can be like having a second job. Is that what you had in mind when you decided to invest in apartment buildings?
- You've got to be able to see potential problems before they arise. Sometimes nothing short of having a crystal ball can help.

In spite of what the gurus say this is *not* the only way to invest in multifamily real estate. I know apartment building investors who have created millions in net worth and built substantial monthly cash flow by buying and holding multifamily properties. In all markets and in all economic times. Sometimes at 15% mortgage rates. These investors have all had a steady, long-term approach to building their real estate portfolios.

One of my friends likes to say, "The bigger pile of gold wins. Would you rather be getting 6% of $100,000 or 6% of $1,000,000?" There's a lot to be said in favor of capital growth. His investment strategy over the years has been "capital growth today, cash as the end game." Buying and holding properties can be a great strategy if you have a good job and you want to keep working. Your income from your job can fund your living expenses while the income from your properties can fund your future real estate investments.

Think twice about your strategies. Don't just do what the gurus say because you think a strategy that works for them is a good strategy for you. Long-term planning can equal long-term rewards. Growing a portfolio of properties and paying off the debt over decades can make you rich.

On the other hand, repositioning properties can be a great strategy. It can even be a ton of fun. To me there's nothing more exciting than seeing a run down, seedy, poorly managed property, realize it's true potential through my efforts.

In this chapter I'll talk about how to successfully renovate and reposition properties. Here's the distinction between renovating a property and repositioning a property:

Renovating a Property

Often times property owners don't address deferred maintenance items such as cleaning and updating common areas with new paint or carpet. A lot of this stuff can be easily fixed at a relatively low cost. Remember though, multiple items like doors and windows can add up quickly. You may be able to improve the landscaping or curb appeal at a property and update common area lighting fixtures and signage without incurring major expenses. These items should be included in your

You want to be sure you have the cash to complete the repairs when you close on the deal.

acquisition budget. In other words, you want to be sure you have the cash to complete the repairs when you close on the deal.

Any large renovation requirements such as new roofs, windows, plumbing, electrical or boilers, should be a part of your negotiations for a seller credit for repairs. You should expect at least 10 years useful life on major building systems when you purchase your property. If those systems need to be replaced today or in the near future, ask for a credit for repairs. If the seller is unwilling to offer a credit for those

> **Expect at least 10 years useful life on major building systems when you purchase your property.**

repairs by lowering the purchase price for the amount of the repair costs I suggest you walk. Let the next guy pick up the tab.

Renovations are simply property improvements such as:

- Fixing up (refreshing) common areas like halls, laundry rooms, mailrooms, stairs, and entryways.
- Improving the property exterior such as adding new land-scaping, painting, lighting, security systems, etc.
- Upgrading individual rental units.
- Replacing, or repairing, major building systems like roofs, boilers, plumbing, electrical, sewer, HVAC, etc.

Repositioning a Property

Repositioning a property primarily refers to management and resident issues. Repositioning is every bit as important as renovating a property and it is often overlooked as a critical part of the VAS.

Making a property beautiful and attractive to current and potential residents is a wonderful and financially smart thing to do. But the last thing you want to do is to spend money on a property and have it full of deadbeat tenants managed by an unskilled management team. Repositioning a property can include some or all of the following:

- Hiring and overseeing a responsive, knowledgeable management team.
- Developing a new marketing plan.
- Changing the reputation of your property.
- Building community.
- Making changes to the current resident base.
- Defining and acquiring your target renter.
- Bringing in a top notch leasing team.
- Resolving any current issues such as poor rent collections and non-responsive maintenance teams and
- Improving the health and well being of your residents by providing a safe and clean living environment.

So Who's in Charge?

Not long ago I read a promotion for an "apartment complex repositioning boot camp." In the sales pitch the guru claimed, "Don't worry about buying a property that needs work. You don't have to do it yourself. You can even live thousands of miles away and be successful. All you need is a team who knows what they're doing!"

Who is this guy trying to kid? This is at best very misleading and at worst dangerous advice. You are the number one person on your team. It is extremely important that you manage your team. Often times this means being on the ground, at the property, taking a critical leadership role throughout the entire process. Think about it. Are you willing to risk a multi-million dollar investment by putting it 100% into the hands of contractors and property managers who have little personal investment in the deal while you live a thousand miles away? When it comes right down to it, the money "your team" is spending on property renovations and on the repositioning of tenants is not coming out of their pockets. It's coming out of yours.

Real estate investing is a business. You are the owner of that business. Always remember you are the one constant member of that business. You're the leader. Teams can and will change. You may fire team members for non-performance from time to time. I've had great teams

> **You're the leader. Teams can and will change.**

who have lost focus. When that happens, they don't always come to you immediately and say, "Hey, we're experiencing some problems here. Things aren't going as planned."

Do you remember Larry from Chapter One? At one time Larry worked for us on a large repositioning project. He was our property manager and renovation partner. We hired Larry because he owned multiple apartment complexes and had successfully repositioned many of those properties. He came to the table with a great deal of expertise. I thought of him as a mentor. But then things started to go wrong. If you'll recall his sister became gravely ill and Larry began traveling out of state to spend time with her. His team stopped working. We quickly started to notice that the units in our building were no longer being turned. The work had virtually stopped on those units. Empty, non-rented units equals zero income. No tenants, no rent payments.

The thing is he never came to me and said, "I'm sorry Theresa. We're not going to make our deadline on turning your units." I discovered it only because I was closely monitoring progress at the property. I visited the property frequently. I walked the units and inspected the work. Unfortunately Larry took his eyes off the ball and failed to communicate with me. In fairness to him his family took priority. In spite of being highly professional with a great deal of integrity, which he was, his priorities changed. His focus was no longer on his business and on the job he was doing for us. And unfortunately in his stress, he failed to communicate any of this to me.

Do you still believe the gurus when they say, "Don't worry, you can be thousands of miles away, all you need is a team who knows what they're doing!" You've heard the saying, "The buck stops with you." It does.

Obviously you can and should establish a system of communication with your team members. You should be getting weekly updates on the work being done at your properties. A word of caution though, even the best systems are vulnerable to human frailties and human nature. You must be a hands-on owner, especially when repositioning properties. It's your business. It's your money.

Get weekly updates on the work being done at your properties.

In the rest of this chapter I'll be covering renovation and repositioning tips learned from the trenches. I've made my share of mistakes and so will you. The trick is to learn and move on quickly.

Renovations: Avoid Single-Family Contractors

Renovating an apartment building is a completely different animal from renovating a single-family home. Typically speaking you won't be renovating apartment units to the high level you would consider for a house. The key with apartment units is to do only what's necessary to command market rents. The only exception to this would be if your strategy is to renovate and market

> **The key with apartment units is to do only what's necessary to command market rents.**

extremely high-end units to an extremely small niche demographic. As I've mentioned I know guys who do this and do it pretty well. This strategy does come with certain risks and in my opinion is more vulnerable to market changes. Market demand is fickle. You are competing with Class A properties for the same amount of rent yet offering an older property with far fewer amenities. It's not a strategy I recommend.

The trick with renovations is to understand your ideal renter and what they are looking for in terms of "sizzle." Then provide it within a reasonable budget. As I've said in my biggest market wood floors are all the rage. It's the first thing a prospective resident asks about when inquiring if we have units for rent. That should be your first clue about market sizzle. What is the number one question out of a prospects mouth?

It might be "Do you have free Wi-Fi? Or in unit washers and dryers?" Markets vary.

I hired a single-family renovator by the name of Walter when I first started out investing in apartment buildings. Like Walter my background in real estate was with single-family homes and small multi-unit properties. After updating the common areas at our very first apartment building, I was pretty excited about moving on to the rental unit upgrades.

We hired Walter to do the work. Walter was used to renovating family houses. He liked installing granite counter tops, new wood cabinetry, tile floors and stainless steel appliances. While I knew better at heart I have to admit it was really tempting to do a high-end renovation.

Before I knew it, my budget of $3,500-4,000 per unit was looking more like $15,000 plus per unit if Walter did the job. I had to let Walter go before we completed the first turn. He simply didn't understand that units in that market were renting for $600 and $800 month for one and two bedroom units respectively *no matter how high-end our renovations were.*

I hate to admit it but I really didn't know what I was doing until I hired a team with apartment building experience. They came in, took a look around the units and suggested very little in terms of renovations. For example the cabinets in the kitchens were a really great 1950's vintage painted metal. I was going to replace all of the cabinets until my team said, "No way. Use this in your marketing as part of the vintage appeal. Besides, those cabinets are easy to paint when a tenant leaves and they stay looking great. Wood cabinets can get damaged."

The other improvements we made to the units were simple. We added new lighting with ceiling fans, painted the units a nice two-tone warm color, refinished the existing wood floors in the main living area and re-carpeted the bedrooms needing new carpet. That's it. No fancy expensive renovations. We even kept the pink and aqua tile in the bathrooms. In fact we left the "vintage charm" throughout the property.

Again the trick is doing just enough to satisfy the market while keeping costs low. The hardest part might just be taking yourself out of it. You are not going to live there. Residents paying $600 month are.

Less is More

As I've said you only want to renovate to a point where you can demand market rents and keep your building at market occupancy. Less is more. Be sure your team has worked on property renovations at the apartment level.

If you run across the guys that want to convince you to go high-end with your improvements talk to the owners they've done this for in the past. Get references. It's a trend I'm seeing more of, especially with "property management" companies. A lot of these guys feel there is not enough skin in the game in simply managing properties so they offer to handle the renovations for you for a price. And a steep price at that. Far more than you would pay by bringing in your own team.

They don't really care about your exit strategies. Or they may attempt to convince you that high-end renovating is the only way to go because you can sell your property at a much higher price based on your high NOI. After all you're getting way above market rents, right? That's the trick. Can you maintain a gross rental income at the high-end in all markets? What if the demand for apartments drops drastically and you end up competing not only with the Class A properties but all other class properties in your market? Watch out for these guys.

The best way to approach your own renovations is to study and know your market intimately. Contact apartment rental leasing agents and property management companies and visit all of the competing properties in your immediate market area. Tour the other properties. Ask about the improvements they've done. Look carefully at the units and at the current renters. Now is the time to completely erase that image in your mind of the perfect apartment for you. Remember, you're not renting an apartment unit for yourself. You are looking to provide what the market wants.

What is the market offering? You can offer just a little more by having the best management team around. By providing responsive, timely maintenance at your properties. By being sure you have a clean, safe environment and decent tenants. You do not have to go hog wild with over the top renovations.

It's All About Income

I was talking the other day with some apartment investors who had decided to hold small, in person seminars for their investment partners and for the owners of the buildings they manage. My friend Mark, who has been a fairly heavy investor in my area over the past decade or so, made a comment that stuck with me.

He said, "Most owners focus on expenses when what they really should be watching is property income." I couldn't agree more. You do not know how many times I've wanted to beat property managers over the head so that they would start thinking in terms of income. It helps to have that mindset. Obviously, if you lower the property expenses your Net Operating Income increases. But start thinking always in terms of income. Ask questions like, "If I spend the money on this particular improvement how will it help increase the income on my property?"

I've had buildings that could use new windows. "Could use" being the operative term. The windows weren't falling out of the frames. They weren't cracked or broken. They were simply older. Newer windows would look better. New windows might even help me with marketing but the bottom line I had to consider was "Where is my renovation money being spent?" "What will give me the best return within my limited budget?"

In the case of the windows it might have made sense to replace them if I was paying all of the utilities. I knew it would be a "green" thing to do. I knew the energy company might possibly offer credits for lowering our utility usage, but it didn't make sense to go in and immediately replace all of the windows. In this property the residents were paying utilities. I suggest you have residents pay their own utilities in all of your properties. When residents are paying for their utilities usage drops. It's a great reason for introducing Ratio Utility Billing Systems (a.k.a. RUBS) at all of the properties you buy. It encourages lower utility usage and increases your bottom line.

We did however replace the roof immediately because the damage presented potential for further water damage to the rest of the property. And I did install a "green" roof. We used a bright, white reflective surface called Durolast and yes, our local energy company offers a credit.

We also installed low cost energy efficient lighting in all of the common areas.

Focus on renovations that can add dollars to your bottom line. Your income. Curb appeal is hugely important and it doesn't take a ton of money to improve a property's appearance. When you can enhance your marketing efforts at a relatively low cost you are doing a good thing. Attracting good residents and keeping your property full should always be a high priority. Don't make the mistake that so many investors make and it seems to happen with many renovation jobs. The investors are willing to spend money on improvements but run out of money before the exterior of the property is updated. Make this a rule for yourself. Start on the exterior updates and curb appeal before you move inside. Exterior renovations can immediately raise your rental price points.

Raising Property Value

As I said at the beginning of this chapter the value of your property is totally tied to the income it generates. You can go in and create that value by increasing the property income and by lowering the property expenses. In a market with a 10% cap rate, you will increase your property value by $10 for each additional $1 in income you generate. Let's use the following formula again:

$$\frac{\text{NOI}}{\text{Cap rate}} = \text{MV}$$

A current NOI of $200,000, at a 10% cap rate, equals a market value of $2,000,000:

$$\$200,000/10\% = \$2,000,000$$

If you increase your NOI by $20,000 you increase your property value by $200,000 as follows:

$$\$220,000/10\% = \$2,200,000$$

This is why some gurus love to promote this strategy. But you need to be careful. If you over improve your property or if you misjudge your expenses going in you can end up sinking a lot more of your money into the deal over the first years of ownership. It follows that this would negate all of that "forced appreciation."

There are many sources of income in an apartment building. Some are overlooked which is why I constantly manage my managers. Some can actually be created where none existed before. For example we had a property with unused but highly efficient individual storage units. I take that back, they were in use but the current on-site manager (who we inherited with the property) had most of the units filled with his stuff. Once we got him to move his items out we offered the units to our residents for $10 per month.

Initially we had no takers. So we began offering the storage units as an incentive, or concession, to our new residents and to our residents who were renewing leases. With each new lease came 3 months use of *free* secure storage units. What do you think happened at the end of 3 months? You got it. The residents didn't want to move their items back out of storage so they gladly started paying $10 month. At 100 units that's an additional $12,000 in annual income or theoretically, an increase in property value of $120,000.

We did the same thing with the covered parking spaces at the complex. Once our residents were used to having an assigned, covered and initially free parking space, they generally started paying for the amenity after the free period expired.

Ways to Increase Gross Operating Income:

Increase rent. You want to buy a property that has legitimate potential upside for increased rents. The rental prices should allow you to "catch up" to the market, not set dramatic new rental records. We discussed those good old "below market rents" in an earlier chapter. It could be true. Some owners intentionally keep rents below market to hold on to tenants. On the other hand you might not even want the current residents. Do your homework.

One thing to take special note of here. Be sure to investigate the current resident and resident leases carefully *before* you buy the property. It is not at all uncommon for property owners to load up, or stuff, a building with poorly qualified tenants in order to make a sale at their target acquisition price.

Some easy rental increases can be accomplished by:

- Cleaning up the building.
- Improving common areas.
- Changing the resident demographic.
- Getting rid of concessions such as free rent. If the market demands rental concessions like free rent or paid utilities, for example, change your offer. How about free parking and storage as an incentive?
- Improving the marketing plan.
- Installing attractive informative signage.
- Replacing current management with a proactive,

courteous team.
- Providing timely maintenance.
- Adding an inexpensive amenity such as a playground.

Raise laundry income. If your complex has a laundry room you can raise the amount of the coin operation. Some properties have a laundry room lease that runs with the property not the seller and most of these leases automatically renew if not cancelled according to contract. Be sure you get a copy of the lease. If you choose to install your own equipment and receive 100% of the laundry income you'll need to cancel the automatic contract renewal per the contract terms.

Add services: It may be possible to install vending machines to common areas. You might also be able to take unused space and create tenant friendly common areas like cafés, office services/business centers and wireless gathering rooms.

Other fees: These are sources of income that can be overlooked such as application, parking and storage fees which can all provide additional income. If your parking area is not full, consider outsourcing it. You might be surprised to discover local businesses will rent parking spaces for their employees.

Utility reimbursement: Have your residents pay utilities whenever possible. You can hire a service company that does this for you or you can charge a flat fee based on unit square footage.

Energy efficiency: You can lower utilities by improving system mechanicals. You can install energy efficient lighting in common areas. As I already mentioned new roofing systems such as Durolast roofing material which is a bright, reflective roofing membrane can lower heating and cooling expenses and some utility companies offer credits for the installation of such systems.

Expenses and Property Improvement Tips

You do not want to discover hidden expenses after you've already bought the property. This should be part of your due diligence. Go back to Chapter Five and take a close look at Exhibit 3. This is a good list of the types of expenses you will incur as an apartment building owner. You will not see this level of detail in the offering brochure but it's your job to know, line item by line item, every single expense you will be paying as an owner.

It is also your job to know how other similar properties perform, or be sure your team has the answers. For example, what is the average cost of property insurance for buildings in your acquisition strategy? What are the typical management fees? Leasing fees? How much do utilities generally run? Taxes? And are the other owners in the area charging utilities back to residents?

After you've analyzed a dozen—or two dozen, or three dozen—deals you will begin to get a feel for common expenses and average price points. This is one of the reasons I have my mentoring students start getting in contract on deals and conducting due diligence. Until you are actually in contract, it's easy to go light on due diligence especially income and expenses. This is why I've made it one of my rules to *always* get the Annual Property Operating Data from the seller of the property. Never rely solely on the numbers the broker gives you.

Never rely solely on the numbers the broker gives you.

One other thought. When you run your analysis on a deal always base it on the current operations of the property *and* on how you will operate the property. Do two sets of analyses. When I make offers on deals I base the offer on the current operations because it helps set a lower offer price. When I talk to my prospective partners, set my exit strategies and determine the property's future value, I base it on how I will improve the property operations.

Ways to Lower Gross Operating Expenses:

- **Contest property tax (reassess).**
- **Shop for a better insurance rate.** Some insurance companies offer 20% off their rates if you belong to certain apartment investor organizations. They may offer discounts for things like improved fire safety systems at your property.
- **Shop all current vendors.** Get competing bids for the service providers such as trash removal, cleaning, landscaping, maintenance, etc. Set up annual reviews for your vendors for both pricing and service. Let them know in advance you'll be doing this so they're expecting it. They should provide better service throughout the year knowing there will be an annual review.
- **Repair and service major buildings systems such as the boiler.** A more efficient boiler means lower utility costs.
- **Go green.** You may receive credits and discounts for installing green energy systems such as roofing, lighting and windows.
- **Lower maintenance and repair costs.** I had a property manager who wanted his electrician and skilled technicians handling all maintenance at my property. Do you

really want to pay an electrician to change a light bulb? Be sure you have the right people doing the appropriate jobs.

- **Build community and inspire tenant retention.** Responsive management, and desirable tenants contribute to a properties' personality. Happy residents equal lease renewals, less turnover and much lower unit make ready expenses.

- **Hold annual reviews for your property management company.** If they are doing their job, they will prepare an annual operating budget for your property. Review budgets annually or even bi-annually. Negotiate fees accordingly. If your company is not meeting expectations, move on.

- **Consider hiring an on-site manager.** A manager with the personality and qualities of your target market can attract good tenants. This can be a great strategy during the repositioning part of your VAS. The cost of a single rent-free unit, say $600 per month, pales in comparison to leasing 15 new units over a 2-3 month period and quickly filling a property with exactly the type of tenant you want living at your property.

- **Complete the following property improvements for better tenant retention and marketing:**
  - » Provide a clean living environment.
  - » Improve resident safety. Install outdoor lighting and secure entryway systems.
  - » Improve curb appeal.
  - » Set community rules and guidelines such as noise free hours.
  - » Make certain your management team is accessible.

If done correctly, it is possible to increase your property value far beyond what normal market appreciation will bring. In Chapter 8 "The Thrill of Negotiations" I'll be discussing negotiating strategies for both acquiring your property and for hiring your team. We'll also go into more detail on leading your team.

CHAPTER SEVEN

✳

Be nice to nerds.
Chances are you'll end up working for one.
—Bill Gates

10-Minute Screening Tools

In this chapter I'm going to explain some quick screening tools—both so you'll know how to use them in your analysis of prospective deals and so you can recognize and use the language with your broker. You'll also be able to use the information obtained from computing these formulas during your negotiations with a seller.

You may want to bookmark this chapter so you can refer back to it easily when you start analyzing your own deals.

We'll be practicing these screening tools with the Exhibits in Chapter 5 "Analyzing the Deal." You can get the exhibits used in this exercise as a free download on my site, www.theresabradleybanta.com/bookdownloads. The more practice you get, the better you'll become at analyzing deals.

Some of these formulas, like the Expense Ratio Formula, will give you an immediate indication of how a property is performing and will also assist you in evaluating how your own property is performing down the road. Others will assist you in figuring out your returns on investment and the likelihood of getting financing.

Let's start with a quick look at some of the terms we'll be using in our ratio calculations:

Potential Gross Income: Also referred to as "Potential Rental Income" or "Annual Gross Rents." This refers to the property's *potential* total rental income at full occupancy.

Effective Rental Income: This is your "Potential Rental Income" less vacancy and credit losses.

Effective Gross Income: This can also be referred to as "Gross Operating Income," "Total Annual Income," "Total Income Collected" and "Total Income." This figure includes all property income such as rent, laundry income, utility income, vending income, parking and storage fees, etc.

Operating Expenses: This can also be referred to as "Total Annual Expenses" and "Total Expenses." These expenses can include management fees, taxes, insurance, repairs and maintenance, utilities, advertising fees, leasing fees, unit make ready costs, accounting and legal fees, landscaping, common area cleaning, trash removal and pest control. Operating expenses do not include debt service.

Net Operating Income (NOI): The total annual income minus the total annual operating expenses (debt service is not included in NOI).

Debt Service: All mortgage payments. Usually this is just principal and interest and does not include taxes and insurance.

Cash Flow: This is the NOI less Debt Service. In other words, rents and other income *minus* expenses, debt and cash reserves.

You can use the following screening tools and formulas to quickly determine if you have any interest in pursuing a multifamily real estate deal. Ready?

Expense Ratio

Simply put, the Expense Ratio is the percentage of the property income that is used to pay expenses. For example if you have an Expense Ratio of 35% this means 35% of your income is going towards the payment of expenses *excluding* debt service. We'll take a look at how to figure out the Expense Ratio in just a minute. But first, let's talk about the significance of this number—because it's an important one.

This is a good formula to use when analyzing a potential deal. You want to know how current expenses compare to income. It is also great for monitoring the performance of your management company after you own a property. In other words, you can use the Expense Ratio as a screening tool for how efficiently a property is being run.

After you purchase a property, and put new management in place, you should see a lower Expense Ratio as a result of improving the property's operations. Your management company should be able to lower your expenses and increase your income. If however, you see your Expense Ratio creeping up after your new management team is on the job, you need to investigate what's going on.

The rule of thumb is that operating expenses on older properties aver-age between 35-45% of Effective Gross Income (all annual property income). The higher the ratio, the less profit for the property owner. The percentage tends to be higher with older buildings because they generally have higher repair and maintenance expenses than new buildings. Here's the formula:

$$\frac{\text{Operating Expenses}}{\text{Effective Gross Income}} = \text{Expense Ratio}$$

Let's take a look at an example using the *Seller Provided Financials* in Exhibit 3 of Chapter Five.

$134,643 (Total Annual Expenses) / $217,056 (Total Income Collected) = .62 (Expense Ratio)

As you can see from this example the Expense Ratio is 62%. This means 62% of the property's total annual income is being spent on expenses. Don't forget, debt service is *not* included in this calculation. You'll also note that this number is significantly higher than the aver-age of 35-45%. Hopefully, you will be able to improve on this number after you purchase the property through better property operations and by increasing the income. If however the current rents are at mar-ket and there is very little upside by increasing rents, you may have a problem.

Now let's look at the numbers the *Broker* provided in Exhibit 2 of Chapter Five:

$107,740 (Total Expenses) / $275,326 (Effective Gross Income) =
.39 (Expense Ratio)

Using the broker's numbers, the property has an Expense Ratio of
39%. We know from our earlier analysis that the brokers are using
favorable numbers in their analysis of the property. So its no great
surprise that the Expense Ratio is quite a bit lower than what you see
when you look at the seller's numbers. Again, it's your job to determine how favorable and how realistic those numbers are.

Just a quick reminder here. Some of the terms you'll see in property
financials are interchangeable, as in the two examples above. For
example, the seller's document refers to total annual property income
as "Total Income Collected" and the broker's Offering Memorandum
uses the term "Effective Gross Income"—these are the same thing.
Refer to the descriptions at the beginning of this chapter if you
aren't sure.

Gross Rent Multiplier (GRM)

This is another quick screening tool. The lower the GRM, the better.
Frankly, I do not rely too heavily on this formula but you will see
it listed in commercial brokers Offering Memorandums and so you
should understand it. This number will vary from market to market,
for example some markets will have a GRM of 8 and others will be
at 13. Take a look at the formula below and then I'll explain how to
use it:

$$\frac{\text{Purchase Price}}{\text{Annual Gross Rents}} = \text{GRM}$$

$2,375,000 (Purchase Price) / $284,040 (Annual Gross Rents) = 8.36(GRM)

Here, the asking price of the property is greater than 8 times the annual rent. Keep in mind this is based on gross rents at full occupancy and does not take other income *or* expenses and repairs into consideration. Don't rely too heavily on the GRM. It is best used when compared to the GRMs of other comparable properties in a single market area. For example, if the average GRM for your market is 8 and you evaluate a property with a GRM of 15, you'll need to investigate the property further. A higher GRM equals less income.

As you begin to review multiple properties in your target market, start to make comparisons between GRMs. As I said, many offering brochures will include the GRM along with the other financial information. Once you become familiar with your market averages, you can use this as a quick screening tool. Is the number too high in comparison with other deals?

Debt Service Coverage Ratio (DSCR)

This is the number lenders use to determine a property's ability to pay the debt service (all mortgage payments). The DSCR is the ratio of cash available to service your debt. A lender *will always* look at this number when they underwrite a property. There are no exceptions. You're going to want to know this number before you approach a lender or a bank about financing your deal. The higher the DSCR the better. On average a lender will want to see a DSCR in the 1.2 to 1.3 ranges. If your deal falls below these numbers you will have trouble financing the property. Here's the formula used to arrive at DSCR:

$$\frac{NOI}{Annual\ Debt\ Service} = DSCR$$

Let's look at the DSCR for the properties from Chapter Five. If we use the numbers from the Seller Provided Financials in Exhibit 3, we have a DSCR of .89, which is a far cry from where it needs to be to gain a lenders approval. Here's the math:

$82,412 (NOI) / $92,619 (Annual Debt Service) = .89 (DSCR)

Remember lenders want to see a number between 1.2 and 1.3 or higher. The higher the number the more able a property is to handle debt service payments. Now using the "estimated" brokers numbers from the offering brochure (Exhibit 2) and let's see what we get:

$167,586 (NOI) / $131,610 (Annual Debt Service) = 1.27 (DSCR)

If in fact the broker's numbers are to be believed, the DSCR falls well within acceptable lenders guidelines. Again, no surprise here, is there? If lenders are looking hard at this number you can bet the brokers are too. Do your own analysis and see where your DSCR is. If it falls well below the acceptable lender standards you will need to adjust (lower) your offering price for the property.

Breakeven Ratio (also called Breakeven Occupancy)

Do you remember at the beginning of this book when I talked about the nightmares that can keep you awake at night? Well, this a good place to remind you. There's nothing worse than owning a property where you get monthly cash calls from your property manager. A "cash call" is when your manager calls you up and says, "Hey I know this isn't really great news but we need $5,000 this month to catch up on expenses." And then you get a call the following month asking for more money. And again. And again. This really can become your worst nightmare.

You can keep these calls to minimum if you understand the Breakeven Occupancy Ratio and if you buy a property that isn't walking a very fine line between cash calls and cash flow. Do you want a property that performs well enough to provide monthly cash distributions to the owner or do you want to get those calls from your manager every month asking for you to fork over even more money?

Here's how the ratio works. If you have a property with a Breakeven Ratio of 100%, you must keep the property at *full* occupancy through-out the entire year in order to break even.

The Breakeven Ratio tells you the percentage occupancy your build-ing must have annually in order to break even after all expenses and debt have been paid. And need I say this? You don't really just want to break even. You want a property that will provide income beyond the break even point. Here's the formula:

$$\frac{\text{Effective Gross Income}}{\text{Operating Expenses} + \text{Debt Service}} = \text{Breakeven Ratio}$$

Let's look at some examples using our favorite property offering again (Exhibit 1, Chapter Five) starting with the Seller Provided Financials in Exhibit 3:

$217,056 (Effective Gross Income) / $134,643 (Total Expenses) +

$$\$92,619 \text{ (Debt Service)} = .95 \text{ (Breakeven Ratio)}$$

This means your property must maintain 95% occupancy annually in order for you to break even. If vacancies move above 5% at any time during the year, you will be taking money out of your own pocket to keep the property running (expenses paid, repairs made). A good rule of thumb is to have a property with a breakeven occupancy allowing for double market vacancy rates. So for example, if your market vacancy is 7.5% you will want to double that (15%) and aim for a breakeven vacancy of 85%, or better.

In the example below, we'll compute the ratio using the broker's numbers from the offering brochure in Exhibit 2. Keep in mind we are not comparing apples to apples because the debt service numbers are not the same. Remember, the brokers are using a debt service number based on the asking price of the property *today*. In other words, you will not be making the same mortgage payments that the current owner makes.

But still this makes for a great comparison:

$$\$275,326 \text{ (Effective Gross Income)} / \$107,740 \text{ (Total Expenses)} +$$
$$\$131,610 \text{ (Debt Service)} = 1.15 \text{ (Breakeven Ratio)}$$

Do you see the difference? In this scenario, the seller's numbers are actually better. Remember, you are looking for properties with a *low* breakeven percentage. A breakeven ratio of 115% simply won't work.

One thing I should note here is that I used Effective Gross Income in my calculations. Again this includes all sources of income such as rent, fees, and laundry. Most property analysts will use the same formula

I gave you. But you can run an even more conservative estimate by using Gross Potential Rent (rent only, no other income) rather than Effective Gross Income in your calculations.

Cash on Cash Return (COC)

This is the percentage return you receive in cash only. It's similar to the rate of interest earned on an investment. We'll use the formulas below in *two steps* to determine your Cash on Cash Return (COC). If you'll recall,

$$NOI - Debt\ Service = Annual\ Cash\ Flow$$

Once you arrive at the Annual Cash Flow on a property, you will use the formula below to figure out your COC Return.

$$\frac{Annual\ Cash\ Flow}{Initial\ Investment} = Cash\ on\ Cash\ Return$$

Now let's do the math. Let's say you have a property that has an annual cash flow of $150,000 (total pre-tax cash received) and your initial investment when you bought the property equaled $1,500,000 (out of pocket):

$150,000 (Annual Cash Flow) / $1,500,000 (Initial Investment) = 10% (COC)

Your cash on cash return is 10%. Let's do one more scenario. Say you buy an apartment building for $2,000,000. You put down 20% to do the deal. In other words your down payment equals $400,000. The property has an annual cash flow of $32,000. Here's how you arrive at your cash on cash return:

$$\$32{,}000 \text{ (Annual Cash Flow)} / \$400{,}000 \text{ (Initial Investment)} = 8.0\% \text{ (COC)}$$

One last thing to note here. If you have closing costs and other out-of-pocket expenses you will want to include those in your initial investment figure. Add these expenses to your down payment for a more accurate COC.

Super Quick Tool to Arrive at a Target Purchase Price

This is a super quick tool you can use to help arrive at a target offering price on a deal. You'll have to know your own market cap rates in order to use it. For a quick refresher on cap rates, refer to Chapter Six "What's a Cap Rate?"

In order to use this tool we'll assume a 50% expense ratio. And we'll use the following Market Value (MV) formula again:

$$\frac{\text{NOI}}{\text{Cap rate}} = \text{MV}$$

You should be familiar with this formula from Chapter Six "Upside."

Ready? Put your thinking cap on. Let's say you have a property with Effective Gross Income of $450,000. This is your total annual income. Let's assume an expense ratio of 50% or $225,000. Remember that most older properties will have an expense ratio of 35-45%. For this exercise we'll use 50% because this will give us a little wiggle room for what we're willing to pay.

The first step is to arrive at our NOI, using the numbers in the example above, as follows:

$450,000 (Effective Gross Income) - $225,000 (Expenses) = $225,000 (NOI)

Don't forget debt service is not included in your NOI. Let's run the MV formula from above using three different market cap rates:

$225,000 (NOI) / .07 (7% Cap) = $3,214,285 (MV or Market Value)

$225,000 (NOI) / .08 (8% Cap) = $2,812,500 (MV or Market Value)

$225,000 (NOI) / .09 (9% Cap) = $2,500,000 (MV or Market Value)

As I said this is a way to quickly arrive at a target offering price. Let's say you're looking at a property with the same NOI from above, $225,000, and the buyers have set an asking price of $4,500,000. If you know that caps in your area should be at 7% on average, then you'll know at a glance that the asking price of $4.5M is extremely high.

One Last Tool: This is One of My Favorites

I've talked about the fancy multifamily analysis software the "gurus" love to give away for "free" (but we know that the price tag is usually the cost of admission to a high-priced boot camp, don't we?). Here's a link to some *free* commercial real estate analysis templates courtesy of Gary Tharp, CCIM. You can download his analysis spreadsheets at www.garytharp.com.

Summary

These are all great screening tools. They are especially powerful when used together. I know many investors who stop short, choosing to use only one or two of the formulas in this chapter. They pick a favorite formula or two and make their buying decisions based on that information. Don't make that mistake. None of these are as powerful alone as they are when used together. With just a little bit of practice you'll become adept at running these ratios quickly. Of course as I've said before, "Garbage in, garbage out." If your numbers are questionable then you are using inaccurate data to determine if deal is a good one or not.

Always understand exactly how the listing broker or seller arrived at their numbers. Get your hands on the actual Annual Property Operating Data from the seller. Carefully review the income and expenses—line item by line item. Lastly, determine how you would run the property before you make a buying decision.

CHAPTER EIGHT

✳

*The fellow who says he'll meet you halfway usually thinks
he's standing on the dividing line.*
—Orlando A. Battista

The Thrill of Negotiations

Everything is Negotiable

Do you remember what my #1 real estate investing money rule is? You
got it. "Everything is Negotiable." One of the reasons I love investing
in real estate is because the opportunities to negotiate are endless.
And I love to negotiate.

You can and should negotiate during every step of the property
acquisition process and also after you've purchased your property. It's
expected. Now is not the time to become a shrinking violet. If you
don't ask, you won't get.

When you buy commercial real estate you may be negotiating with all
of the following:

- Brokers.
- Sellers.
- Contractors (rehab and maintenance teams).
- Service providers and vendors (trash company, insurance companies, etc.)
- Title companies.
- Lenders.
- Property managers.
- Attorneys.
- Property inspectors.
- Tax professionals
- Equity partners, if any.
- Prospective residents at your property.

One of the reasons I generally work only with mentoring students who have had prior real estate investing experience is because they've already pulled the trigger on a property. This usually means they've bought and sold single-family investment properties. They've learned to negotiate deals on a smaller level and they "get" that negotiation is an important part of the process.

With any real estate transaction, you *must* negotiate. Especially when you are spending several million dollars on a property and possibly an additional couple hundred thousand on renovations. You've got to get over the fear that you might insult someone. You need to be comfortable with the process. Negotiations do not need to be adversarial. They go much more smoothly when they're not, read on and you'll see why.

In this chapter I'll give you some examples that will help illustrate how to negotiate with:

- Your property manager (and anyone else you hire to work for you).
- The seller of the property that you want to acquire (and by default, your broker).

My intent is that you start to become more comfortable with the negotiation process, especially because you will be working with much larger numbers. We'll also talk about how you can make sure your team understands that they work for you and not the other way around.

The First Thing to Remember About Negotiations

I approach every single negotiation the same way. It's a technique I learned from one of my mentors years ago and it works. This strategy almost always assures that your negotiations are successful and it's a great way to take the pressure of negotiating off of your back.

I've used this technique for every investment property I've ever acquired and I went as far as using it when my husband and I purchased our personal residence. Some might say that's taking things a little bit far but it worked. We bought a home we love at a great price and the seller repaired every item on our inspection list.

Here's what you do:

Let's start with a money rule okay? Never, ever fall in love with investment real estate before you buy it. *Ever.* We talked about this earlier in the book. You must have a tight acquisition strategy that you do not deviate from. The numbers have to work. The location or market has to be right. You must know what type of property you want to buy.

The reason this is critically important will become clear in a minute.

When you negotiate, you absolutely have to convey to the other party that you are willing to walk away from the deal. They must clearly understand that you don't need to do the deal, that you have plenty of other options, that you are not in love with the property, that this is strictly an investment and that there are plenty more deals out there. The trick to this strategy is that you've got to really and truly believe this yourself or the other party will never buy it. This is pretty hard to carry off if you've fallen head over heels in love with a property.

> **You absolutely have to convey to the other party that you are willing to walk away from the deal.**

When we bought our home, the truth is I *had* fallen a little bit in love with it when we first looked at it. This was a property we were going to live in and it met with almost all of our acquisition requirements. Yep, we had a list of the things our new home must have. We also knew the sellers were very motivated. They had just finished rehabbing the property when 9-11 happened and then they were forced to sit on it for several years, even renting it out to a family for a short time. But knowing the rules of negotiation, I knew I had to convey to the seller that we were in fact absolutely willing to move on if our terms would not be considered.

The seller's original asking price was based entirely on how much money they had put into improvements. They were looking to make a profit even though the market had declined while they attempted to sell the property at the previous market price. Plus they were losing money on the house every day in carrying costs. In addition I knew that the seller had financial problems. Using my negotiation strategy we certainly risked losing the house but when we indicated that we were willing to walk the seller agreed to our terms.

Additionally, the sellers knew full well that they had stopped short in rehabbing the property. As typical of many single-family flippers, they had run out of funds for all exterior improvements. Some chimneys needed repairs. The landscaping was non-existent. I knew I could use all of this to my advantage in negotiations. We were dealing with a very motivated seller. Even so, this was probably the hardest deal I ever negotiated because we really wanted the house and I hated to risk losing it.

Keep this story in mind as you think about just how badly you want to acquire a particular property. It's just as easy to fall in love with the idea of ownership, as it is to fall in love with a property. You've got to step back and think long and hard about your motivation. Ask yourself these questions, "Does this property meet all of my requirements? Will I be making a wise investment at this asking price?"

You've got to step back and think long and hard about your motivation.

If the answer is "No" move on. I talked earlier about negotiating a seller credit for repairs. If an apartment building needs major repairs such as a new boiler or roof and you cannot get the seller to credit the cost of those repairs against the acquisition price, be willing to pass on the deal and let the next guy pick it up and pay the costs. There are always more deals.

State your case clearly. The seller is very aware of where their property falls short. They know when deferred maintenance has not been addressed. It will come as no great surprise when you say, "This is a pretty good property and your asking price is reasonable, but as the owner I will have to make improvements to the major building systems. I can't justify paying your asking price and paying for the cost of those improvements too. If we can't agree on a credit then I'm afraid I will just have to pass on the opportunity."

Remember you're not hoping they'll agree to a credit. You're coming from a place of "Oh well, I guess this deal is not the one for me. It doesn't make fiscal sense." Don't come from a place of having fallen in love with the deal. Keep your emotions out of it and deal strictly with the numbers.

Your Team: They Work For You!

In Chapter Three I talked about another one of my money rules: "Your broker works for you. It's not the other way around."

I was telling you about how I instructed my broker Bob to bring an offer to the seller even though he felt the offer was way too low. Actually what I said was: I made an offer and "my broker almost choked when he heard it."

The sellers were asking $1,890,000 for their property. I offered $1,600,000. Almost $300,000 less than what they wanted. I remember my broker saying, "I can't take that price to them. They'll never accept it." So I patiently explained to Bob how I had arrived at the price. The numbers didn't support an offer above $1.6M.

Then Bob called and said, "You're not going to believe this! The sellers accepted. They signed the contract!"

After completing due diligence on the property, while still in contract, I asked Bob to present a request for an additional $60,000 credit for repairs. Again, he balked but did as I asked. And once again, the seller accepted. We purchased the property for a total of $1,540,000. We also got the sellers to agree to carry back an interest only, unsecured (not backed by the property) promissory note for $100,000.

Why did I start with such a low offer? Based on my financial analysis it was a fair offering price. Once we inspected the property and discovered undisclosed deferred maintenance, my request for a credit was not out of line either. Just don't go crazy with your requests, okay? You don't want to ask the

Always inspect a property for undisclosed deferred maintenance.

seller to do things like install a fancy canopy over the main entrance. We're talking deferred maintenance, necessary things that need to be repaired or replaced.

Secondly, I knew the history of the sellers. They had inherited the property and pretty much let it decline during their ownership. I knew that their level of motivation to sell was high. They weren't selling "their baby." They were simply looking forward to a large profit at the closing table. It was a windfall for them because they had invested absolutely nothing in the deal including their own personal time or energy.

So, here's another acquisition strategy or rule while I'm on the subject: Always find out why the seller is truly selling.

I usually ask, "So, tell me, why exactly is the seller selling their property?" I ask this question at least four times. The first time you usually get some incomprehensible answer about why the seller is selling. Rarely is it the real reason. The second time you ask, you demonstrate that you really do want an answer to your question. Be circumspect,

Always find out why the seller is truly selling.

insert inquiries into your conversation naturally such as, "So I didn't quite get it, why are they selling?" By the third and fourth time you ask, it becomes increasingly difficult for the broker to give you a vague explanation. The real story eventually comes out and you can almost always use the information in your negotiations.

So, why did Bob hesitate to bring the offer? I may never know. Bob is actually a really great guy and a fantastic broker. Perhaps he thought he risked losing the deal because I was insulting the seller. Or maybe he had decided I didn't know what I was talking about. The bottom line however is this. I did know what I was doing and more importantly, I knew that Bob worked for me. I offered what I was willing to pay and it was his job to present the offer to the seller. Fortunately over the years we've developed a good relationship. Bob's rarely surprised anymore when I speak my mind. He advises and he listens. It makes for a good team.

Let's talk about Bob, and negotiations, some more. Bear in mind as you read this, that I really do like the guy, okay? Otherwise you might begin to wonder why I work with him. He's smart. He really knows the market. And he brings good deals to my attention. Not stuff that's been shopped around town to every broker and good buddy before I see it. I always learn stuff from Bob too. He might even be a more dedicated student of the industry than I am. And that's saying a lot.

Building strong relationships with people who take their business very seriously is a smart thing to do.

Bob's generally good for some educational stories too. And now that I think about it, this story might illustrate that negotiations aren't exactly Bob's strong suit. You probably know about playing the high-low game in negotiations.

Generally the high-low game is started with the seller taking an unreasonable position with their asking price. Then the buyer is expected to offer a lowball counter to the sellers opening gambit. The seller then responds with a price that is lower but still significantly higher than where they expect to end.

Ultimately what usually happens is that relationships become irrevocably damaged to the detriment of all because nobody ends up feeling as though they've won.

I listed an apartment building with Bob last year. Our asking price was $2,100,000. I had no intention of playing the high-low game during negotiations because of the damaging nature of the game and I made this very clear to Bob. I set a fair asking price and let Bob know we were willing to negotiate down to $2,050,000—at $2.1M we would have been very happy, at $2.05M the buyers got a great deal. Pretty much a win-win all the way around.

We received an offer of $1,900,000 and we countered with $2,075,000.

The buyers came back with a new counter of $1,925,000 and we told Bob to let them know that would we would go no lower than $2,050,000. Period. The price was supported by the property condition. It was a turnkey property after all. The price was also supported by the property financials. It was a fair price. I also told Bob, "Hey, we don't have to do this deal. There are other buyers out there." Remember, always convey to the other parties that you are more than willing to walk away from a deal.

Suddenly Bob suggested, "Why don't you meet the buyer halfway at $1,987,500?"

Now wait a minute, if we were to meet the buyer "halfway" we would have agreed to a price of $2,000,000, right? We were asking $2,100,000 and the original offer from the buyer was $1,900,000. By my math halfway is $2,000,000.

It became immediately obvious that the buyers broker was playing the game. He was telling the buyer, "Gosh, they won't even meet you at the halfway point!"

He was trying to be very creative with the math by using the new counter pricing instead of our original asking price and he was using it against us. Do you see the difference? At the last point in the negotiations we were at $2,075,000 and the buyers were at $1,925,000. "Halfway" would now be $1,987,500.

We weren't really being asked to meet halfway. They were asking us to meet at a new imaginary mid-point, derived from the ongoing counter offers. Pretty tricky.

He was telling the buyer we were inflexible and stubborn by not meeting them halfway. After all halfway is only fair isn't it? Suddenly we became the bad guys. Negotiations were no longer "fair."

Here's where Bob came in. He thought we should accept this new "creative" in-between price. Until I said, "Tell the buyer 'no deal'. And you can tell the buyer's broker that we don't appreciate the games he's playing. No one wins in this scenario and the broker is damaging the relationships of all the parties involved here."

Unfortunately, an impasse had been reached or so I thought at the time. And that's the risk of playing the high-low game. What could have been a working, interest based negotiation turned into an adversarial contest. Frequently in this scenario nobody wins.

Bob became a little embarrassed and defensive when I called him on this. Do you see how this type of negotiation can damage other aspects of relationships? I was not happy with Bob for his willingness to play this game especially since I had stated at the beginning that I had no intention of doing so.

The good news is both brokers backed off from their negotiating strategies. We did sell the property to those buyers at the price we wanted. We had a pleasant conversation at the closing table.

Hiring Team Members

I've hired my share of commercial property managers. Most markets have standard pricing. For example you can assume that you will pay a 5-7% management fee plus leasing fees to the manager of your property. Even so, negotiations are important. Each management company will have small differences and you need to drill down to find out how their team members are paid. No two companies have the same fee arrangements.

Remember when I asked you if you want to pay an electrician to change a light bulb at electrician's prices? When you first sit down and meet with a prospective manager and this applies to contractors too, ask to read a copy of their management agreement or contract. I'll tell you this; every single management agreement I've seen is about 15 to 30 pages long. I won't even read them any more. Instead I use a straight-forward two-page document that covers everything succinctly. I also add an arbitration clause which basically states: "Any controversy or claim arising out of or relating to the interpretation or application of any provision of this Agreement shall be settled by mediation and/or binding arbitration." This replaces the standard language that usually ends up with you, the property owner, paying for all attorneys' fees. Arbitration is in my opinion the 21st century way of doing business. Each party gets a fair hearing in front of an impartial arbitrator. It's a give and take exchange. In my experience most parties walk away feeling good about the outcome.

Bottom line? You do not have to use the contracts provided by your vendors.

Some of these contracts are actually a cut-and-paste compilation of everything anyone has ever told a company to cover. Their friends, family and maybe a lawyer gets thrown in the advice mix. Some are boilerplate contracts that even the management company doesn't understand. Even a boilerplate contract can be changed. It's a place to start. It is not the ending. It may seem black and white because that's the nature of the typewritten word on paper. But sometimes outcomes are best found in what's not written. Terms can be re-written and new language can be introduced,

You do not have to use the contracts provided by your vendors.

making for a far less confrontational negotiation.

One time I was in the middle of negotiating a contract with the owner of a property management company. His name was Douglas. We were on our third meeting, partly because I was still interviewing him but also because he had this tome of a management contract. He in fact admitted he hadn't read the whole thing

Terms can be re-written and new language can be introduced.

and didn't understand it all. I knew we had to simplify things. Additionally, his pricing was a little non traditional. Douglas was the guy with the electrician who changed light bulbs and it was my intention to make sure we were not paying $40 an hour for general, simple maintenance.

In our earlier meetings we sat across a big conference table from each other. But at our third meeting, as we entered the conference room I said, "Let's sit next to each other."

His response? "Wow, by sitting next to each other this will be a lot less adversarial." What he said was exactly right. It was also a bit of a red flag. He was expecting an adversarial meeting? Why? Turns out that little niggling feeling I got when he made that comment was right because this guy did turn out to be a confrontational and an angry kind of guy. You should really listen to your intuition.

I was approaching the negotiations as if we were on the same team. My decision to hire him was already made. I knew that together we were going to decide on terms that we both liked. So, I suggested we sit next to each other as if we were already working together. As if we were already on the same team. I wanted him to get the same idea.

I didn't come to our meeting thinking, "I'm going to get everything I want." I showed up with some flexibility in mind that made it possible for both of us to leave with a signed contract. Terms that surprised and pleased him. His response? "This worked out great and I'm going to steal your ideas to use with my other clients." We ended up with a short, concise understandable management agreement. You'll find an example in the Appendix of this book.

So the lesson here is this:

- You do not have to use the agreement or contract provided by the service provider. You have every right to change the contract language and the terms of the agreement.
- Approach negotiations as if you're on the same team. In reality you are. If things go smoothly and the company performs well, you may be working together for years to come.
- Trust your intuition when dealing with people. Remember, they are not the only service provider out there. It's okay to take your time and find the person who is the right fit for you and your business.

I'll talk more in the next chapter about hiring a team. About who should be on your team and how to keep the right mindset about who is in charge.

CHAPTER NINE

*

The task of the leader is to get his people from where they are to where they have not been.
—Henry Kissinger

You Are the Team Leader

You Do Not Jump Through Hoops for Your Team

In the last chapter I talked about Bob, my broker. He's one of several brokers I really like to work with—partly because he likes to tell me exactly what he thinks, but mostly because he actually listens. Having a broker act as an intermediary between you and a seller, or between you and a buyer, can be priceless. It can soften your dealings with the other party by having your broker act as your "diplomat."

But sometimes you have to remind them that they work for you. I had a mentoring student, Allen, who told me about an experience he'd just had working with a broker in his market.

He'd contacted the broker and let him know that he was an active investor in very small multifamily properties and he wanted to move into larger deals. Sound familiar? What Allen said was absolutely true. At the time he owned about 12 units and he was doing pretty well with those small properties.

I'm not usually surprised by what I hear, but this surprised me. Allen was told by his commercial real estate broker to meet with his banker and get pre-qualified for a loan before he would show him any deals.

Here's the thing I really want you to know. I listened to my mentor and my first deal was in the neighborhood of $2,000,000. If you'll recall, my mentor taught me that money *always* finds great deals. So I looked at big deals. If Allen had taken his broker's advice he was more than likely on his way to acquiring a property for $200,000 or less.

Money always finds great deals.

Getting pre-qualified for a loan is not a terrible idea, especially if you're buying a single-family property but it's extremely time consuming. In addition the chances of you actually getting a loan for an apartment building from a private bank aren't great. The likelihood of this happening is rare unless you have a long-term, close relationship with your banker or you have a great deal of cash on deposit at the bank. Plus the bank must actually want to include multifamily properties in its portfolio. Some banks don't even have experience with this type of lending.

But, here's the main problem with this idea of getting pre-qualified. And it's a big one.

By telling Allen to get pre-qualified for a loan, his broker limited Allen's thinking exponentially. He pretty much told Allen that he had to have all the funds personally to close on a deal. And depending on how much cash and borrowing ability Allen had, his broker narrowed the available properties tremendously.

If you only have $50,000 to invest, by default you are now looking at small deals. And instead of a hundred deals, you're now looking at only about 4 or 5. You end up thinking small. You may become discouraged by what your banker tells you.

The truth is when you find an incredible deal, the money part of it is easy. People are delighted to invest in profitable deals. I'm going to ask you to take a leap of faith here. Once you have a number of deals under your belt you will see that this is true. What's unfortunate is that Allen's broker needlessly put him in a fearful position. Instead of supporting Allen in thinking in terms of abundance, Allen was now thinking about scarcity. You cannot grow a successful business if you think about what you can't do. In order to succeed you have to focus on reaching and achieving your goals. And those goals should be a stretch for you.

When I work with brokers I lead the process. I let them know clearly with no misgivings or misunderstandings, that our relationship is about their finding me great deals. Period. I know for a fact that money always follows great deals. It doesn't matter if I personally qualify or not. When my broker presents an incredible deal, getting the investment funds needed to do the deal isn't a problem. Most people are thrilled to have the opportunity to take funds out of an account that is earning 0-5% and put it to work in an investment earning much higher returns.

You can spend a tremendous amount of time talking to a single bank, getting all your paperwork together and filling out applications. Ultimately the bank might not even finance your deal. This is not what your relationship with your broker should look like—at all. Your broker should not be directing you to meet with your banker. A broker might assist you by giving you the names of the financial institutions that are big players in your local multifamily market. Ask for referrals and the names of people you can speak to. This is a great way for your broker to assist you.

You will find a sample "real estate resume" in the Appendix of this book. This is a document you will want to prepare before you talk to lenders. Lenders are likely to ask for it. It's a simple one-page statement of experience that will show lenders you have some education and experience with real estate investing and that you have the right people on your team.

If your experience in real estate investing is light, you absolutely want to include your team members. Lenders want to know for example that you have a professional management company on board, ready and prepared to take over your new apartment building. Some lenders may even make this a requirement for your first year of ownership.

Tire Kickers

I'm sure one of the reasons Allen's broker had him run over to meet his banker and get pre-qualified for a loan is that he most likely didn't take Allen very seriously. Even though Allen already owned several investment properties. Most brokers, at least the brokers that I know personally, find that single-family real estate investors are tire kickers.

They may have a strong desire to move into bigger deals but they rarely do so. There's a lot of truth to this. I see it happen with the students who graduate from real estate boot camps, especially those who try to go it alone without working directly with mentors in the business. It's easy to become scared into inaction when you know you know only enough to be dangerous. When you play a bigger game you can make vastly bigger mistakes. Very costly mistakes.

This is exactly why I invested in team, multifamily mentors and deal-makers when I first moved from single-family investing into multi-family investing. I didn't want to make huge mistakes. I also knew that I wanted to lead my team and in order to do that I needed to know

> **You will always need a team no matter how much experience you gain by investing in deals.**

what I was doing. I'm not saying you have to know everything, but you do need to know what you don't know so that you can get the right team members working with you. You will always need a team no matter how much experience you gain by investing in deals.

So, back to the brokers. Some brokers are reluctant to present deals to investors who may never make offers on deals. Tire kickers. And who can blame them? Brokers invest a lot of time working with prospective buyers. They don't want to work with investors who will never enter into a deal or will back out of a deal because of fear.

It's your job to get the brokers you contact to decide you are the exception to the rule. How do you do that? You've got to be gutsy. You must get enough education so that you have a solid plan. And you've got to start making offers on properties. Put your fear aside and get into the action. The question you should be asking yourself right now is, "Why would I try to do this without a mentor guiding me?" If you want to succeed in this business, you've got to take action. But you don't have to do it alone. I didn't. You shouldn't either. Building relationships with and hiring a mentor is the best money you will ever invest.

Now, here's a flip side to this story. When I first started out I contacted a lot of brokers. I was trying to find a broker whom I thought I could work with, someone who matched my style of doing business. Somebody I felt I could trust. Once they took me seriously (yes, I was one of those single-family investors looking to buy my first apartment building) they started calling me about listings. "Hey, let's go take a look at this property!" they'd say. And I did. It was a lot of fun, for a while.

But it didn't take long to figure out that some of these showings were a complete waste of my time. Some of the properties did not meet my money rules or investment acquisition strategies and were, frankly, overpriced. They were not great deals. They'd already been shopped around. Also, these showings were very time consuming. Ultimately I had to say, "I can't spend my time at showings on marginal properties. I'll take a look at the listing memorandum but I also want the seller's numbers before I decide to take a trip to the property." This sounds like a money rule we talked about in Chapter Five!

The Players

The following is a list of the people you'll want on your team. You'll also find a list of the people you want to have on your team in the Appendix. They do not all have to be in place immediately, but you should have each one identified and selected before you need them.

Actually it's even better to start assembling a list now. Use the checklist in the Appendix of this book. Don't wait to find someone until you need them. The best way to do this is via referrals or known contacts. Your commercial real estate broker will know many of the players in the multifamily arena. Your mentor will too.

Notice I said "commercial real estate broker". Your local residential realtor is unlikely to have referrals of service providers to the *multi-family industry*. Be careful that you understand the difference. Your realtor might know a great property inspector but chances are slim to none that that person has inspected an apartment building. This is why you need to build your list via your networking in the multifamily industry.

There are membership organizations specific to the apartment industry such as *The National Apartment Association* (www.naahq.org). You might also have apartment associations at the local level. These can be a good source of vendors and suppliers. But I've found the best referrals come via word of mouth. They are referred by people in the industry that you know and trust. Especially your contractors like roofers, electricians, plumbers etc. You want trades people who have worked specifically on apartment building systems. Don't hire your local single-family guys. Just don't do it. They have no idea how to work on apartment building systems or how to keep repairs and renovations in line with the property's ability to earn income.

Your team:

- Mentors.
- Inspector(s): This includes commercial real estate inspection services and structural engineers.

- Commercial Real Estate (Multifamily) Broker.
- Attorney.
- Title Company.
- Commercial Lenders: Your broker may have some good referrals for this. Look for lenders who are actively financing apartment deals in your market.
- Equity Partners.
- IRA Custodian.
- Property Manager: Companies experienced in managing multifamily properties.
- CPA, Bookkeeper.
- Tax Strategist.
- 1031 Exchanger: At some point you may wish to exchange your investment into another property and defer capital gains tax payments (1031 Exchange).
- Insurance.
- Rehab/Maintenance: Work with the people who have successfully renovated apartment buildings.

The Mystery of Property Managers

And now, I saved the best team member for last—your property manager. On the one hand you'll love them and on the other you might despair of them ever doing a really great job for you. The following should help. I've also included a list of interview questions for you to use when hiring a property manager in the Appendix of this book.

Having a property management company on your team allows you to manage your asset rather than the property. In other words you are not paying the bills, creating the books, marketing or leasing units and overseeing daily maintenance at the property. It frees you up to stay current on your local market, to make decisions about selling or refinancing your property and to look for more deals so you can grow your portfolio and your business. Let your team work in the business by handling the daily operations so you can work on your business. Do you see the distinction?

You are responsible for managing the manager. You are the one who will be overseeing the activities of every member of your team. One of the best things you can do is set up the systems by which you will communicate. I like to do everything by email so there is a paper/electronic trail. I'm a big texter, but I keep that for friends and family. With my management teams I do everything in writing. I keep a paper trail for everything.

My managers give me weekly written reports on the smaller activities at the property such a leasing updates. They are also responsible for providing the monthly operating data such as Cash Flow Statements, Balance Sheets, General Ledgers and Rent Rolls. I also request that these reports are kept current and are available to me whenever I ask for them. Most companies use online systems that can be accessed by the owner of the property. Make sure you request this access.

My management company is also responsible for creating and updating an Annual Property Operating Budget. These are projections for income and expenses throughout a given year. It's a good idea to review these projections against current market reality on a *quarterly* basis.

Your job is to review all of the financials. Don't leave it to your manager to summarize what's going on at your property. You must look at income and expenses regularly. It is critical that you review leasing updates and the property Rent Roll regularly. Like every week.

Property managers often only see what's in front of their noses. At one point we had a property where the debt service (mortgage payment) was being paid out of the owners operating account. Normally this debt will be paid out of the property operations account. This is the bank account the property manager uses for collecting all income and for paying property expenses. But we had just switched management companies and we were temporarily paying debt service from a separate account.

Guess what happened? Our manager was using cash flow statements *sans debt service*. What he saw was a property that was throwing off a ton of cash because his reports and bank account did not include our debt service payments. What do you think happens when your manager thinks the property is performing beyond his wildest dreams? He takes his eye off the ball. Leasing becomes less important. He starts to believe there is a ton of excess cash for little property improvements here and there.

Throughout those three or four months while we paid our own debt service payments, I was constantly telling Douglas our erstwhile manager, "Don't forget we are paying the mortgage invoices, Douglas. The property is not performing quite the way you think it is."

But like I said, sometimes your manager will only see what's right in front of his/her nose. The bottom line is this, it is your job to guide and oversee your manager. To request frequent updates. And to let your manager know you want to be actively involved.

Managers can also overlook income opportunities. Let's face it. Many managers don't own their own apartment buildings so they don't think like owners. It's your job to be sure they do. For example, be sure they are renting your storage units and renting out the parking spaces

> **Many managers don't own their own apartment buildings so they don't think like owners.**

in addition to renting a unit. Monitor the types of concessions they are offering to prospective residents. Concessions like free rent or lowered security deposits can be replaced with free parking or storage. Or you can offer your residents incentives for referring their friends and family as prospective renters. If they help you lease a unit, you give them a small discount on one month's rent. Strategize with your team on ways to offer creative concessions without costing you income.

Find out how often the laundry is being used and discuss what can be done to encourage the residents to use it more frequently. It might be something simple like making sure the laundry room is being cleaned nightly. Sometimes you have to help or train your manager to learn to think like an owner.

Lastly, don't let emotions rule your relationship with your team members. I let my managers and other contractors know there will be annual performance reviews. They also know there's a bonus for them if they perform well. Set the scene at the beginning of your relationship. Be willing to pull the plug early, not later. If a manager is simply not performing, move on.

****

You know the gurus will tell you anyone can buy, own and operate apartment buildings. They love to say, "The beauty of buying and owning apartment buildings is that you are not doing the work yourself. No calls from tenants in the night crying about plugged up, overflowing toilets. Just a bunch of tenants [implied: faceless, unimportant tenants] who are paying for your investment. While you sit back and collect the dough."

I hope after reading this book you realize things are a lot more complicated and involved than that view point. Apartment building ownership is not for everyone. But residential multifamily real estate does have its rewards. You have an opportunity to be the type of investor who cares for the happiness and welfare of others. You can provide a safe and attractive environment for your residents. A place they call home. The financial rewards can be great too.

CHAPTER TEN

✳

Sow a thought, reap an action; sow an action, reap a habit;
sow a habit, reap a character; sow a character, reap a destiny.
—*Chinese Proverb*

Conclusion

I hope that you've found tremendous value in this book. It was my goal to give you true and actionable information. It is also my goal to stress how important it is that you do not go it alone as you build your multifamily investment business.

As you can see there's a lot of bad advice out there and you can't afford to make mistakes at this level. Build a great team. Become a student of the industry. Learn as much as you can but don't sit on the sidelines either.

A Typical Real Estate Investor's Road to Investing

The flow charts below outline the typical path most people take to get into the commercial real estate arena. As you read them, keep in mind there are alternatives. Do you remember my mentor who showed me the clock face to help illustrate just how much I knew—or didn't know—about real estate investing? He loved to say, "Over half of what you don't know about investing in real estate, *you don't know you don't know*."

Just think about that for a minute. When you really get what he's saying, it's almost enough to make you give up. So ask yourself this. How can any boot camp, book or webinar alone help you as an *individual*?

They can't.

My goal in writing this book is to give you not only an overview of investing in multifamily real estate, but to help you identify your own personal beliefs and paradigms about success. Your personal success. Take a minute and do a self-assessment.

- What areas will you need the most work in to be a success?
- What do you already know?
- What things are truly going to allow you to play a much bigger game?
- What might stop you from playing a bigger game?

Here's where most people start:

Decide It's Time To Invest In Multifamily Real Estate
Make a Commitment and Set Some Goals!

Start Reading Books On:
Real Estate Investing & Buying Apartment Buildings

"Discover" a Real Estate Guru
Buy DVDs, Workbooks, Audio Recordings

Revaluate Their Decision
Fear, Apprehension & Self-doubt Set In

So now they've invested a lot of time only to say, "Whoa, maybe this isn't such a great idea. I'm not even sure where to start."

They pause and then they decide to start by dipping their toe in the water.

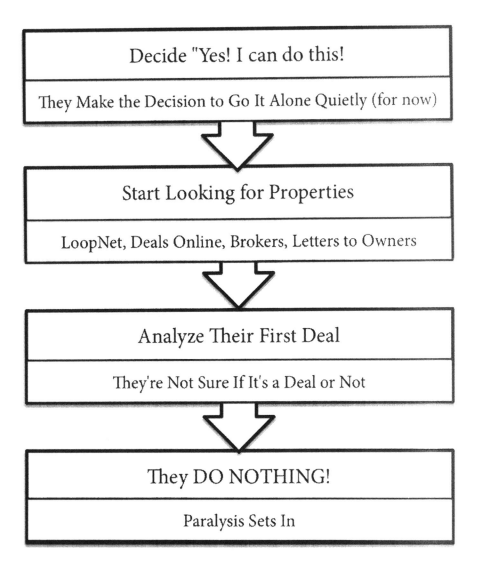

Once again, they're right back at the drawing board.

Doing things quietly and on their own hasn't gotten them very far. They start wondering if they really need some help outside of the research that they've been able to do on their own. It's time to take serious action.

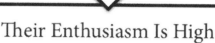

Attend a Multi-day Seminar

They Finally Fork Over the Big Bucks

Their Enthusiasm Is High

They Join a Real Estate Club, Talk to Potential Partners

NOW They're Ready to Get Serious

They Cannot Decide Where to Begin

They Decide to Wait

The "Timing is Off", The "Market's Not Right"

If this is you you are not alone. This is such a typical route for most people who decide to get in the multifamily investing game. But what if there was another way?

How do you skip this process all together?

This is What You Do

If you are getting ready to invest tens if not hundreds of thousands of dollars in multifamily real estate, doesn't it make sense to invest a small percentage of those dollars in your education first?

Here's your next step. Invest in a mentor. Work with experienced real estate investors. Re-read this book and make special note of the areas where you might need support. Keep the flow charts in mind. Where do you typically get hung up?

Use the Real Estate Investor Self-Assessment Questionnaire in the back of this book. Take some time to fill it out. Really think about your answers.

Once you've filled out your personal assessment go to my website www.theresabradleybanta.com/contact and contact me to schedule your *free* 30-minute strategy session.

Appendix: Forms and Documents

All of the exhibits, documents and forms used in this book and in the Appendix are available for free download at www.theresabradley-banta.com/bookdownloads.

****

Where are you right now?

Where do you want to be?

The following questionnaire and assessment will help you discover your strengths and will greatly assist you in figuring out where you want to go on your real estate investing journey.

This is a great tool to identify your strengths and to recognize the areas you really want to tweak. It will also help *you* lead your mentor on your journey.

Please give yourself permission to be completely honest as you answer each question.

Appendix A: Investor Self-Assessment Questionnaire

Name: _____

Date: _____

Please evaluate yourself on the statements below using the 1-10 scale (1 = low, 10 = high):

_____ I am confident in the areas of money and finance.

_____ I have prior real estate investing experience.

_____ I have clear goals for my real estate business.

_____ I can invest a significant amount time in my real estate business.

_____ I'm willing to work hard to achieve my goals.

_____ I know how to analyze real estate deals.

_____ I have the confidence to make deals.

_____ I have an experienced team of real estate professionals.

_____ I have strong leadership skills.

_____ I surround myself with talent and get out of their way.

_____ I am a positive thinker and approach problems creatively.

_____ I'm not afraid to network.

_____ I set goals and meet them.

_____ I can easily get rid of the excuses that hold me back.

_____ I am open to new ideas.

_____ I want to play a bigger game.

_____ I do not engage in limiting self-talk.

_____ I stay cool in a crisis.

_____ I'm able to stay focused on my dreams and vision of the future.

_____ I have no trouble overcoming the fear of success or failure.

_____ I want to make significant changes in my life.

I would like the primary focus of my growth to be on:
(choose one)

_____ Working on my goals and vision and belief in my own success.

_____ Strictly real estate investing education, I already know how to achieve goals.

What is your purpose for investing in real estate?

_____

_____

_____

_____

What are your goals?

_____

_____

_____

What are your specific expectations from a mentor?

_____

_____

_____

In what areas do you currently feel stuck?

_____

_____

_____

When you are stuck, frustrated, discouraged, or in resistance, what do you usually do?

_____

_____

_____

What qualities do you look for in the people you hang out with?

_____

_____

What level of determination and commitment will you bring to the table in order to succeed as a real estate investor?

_____

_____

_____

What motivates you and what doesn't?

_____

_____

_____

What would you do with your time once you no longer have to work for money?

_____

_____

_____

What would you do as a means of giving back when you become financially independent?

_____

_____

_____

How do you bring courage and conviction to risky situations?

_____

_____

_____

What do you do to challenge your underlying beliefs, paradigms and assumptions?

_____

_____

_____

How would you describe your personal work style and pace?

_____

_____

_____

Do you plan to hire team? If so, who?

_____

_____

_____

What type of leader are you?

_____

_____

_____

What does working 'on' your business mean to you?

_____

_____

_____

How many real estate deals have you done? (please describe)

_____

_____

_____

Describe your current real estate portfolio.

_____

_____

_____

How many deals have been successful?

_____

_____

_____

How much money do you have available to invest in real estate?

_____

_____

_____

Have much time do you have to devote to your business?

_____

_____

_____

When do plan to work (e.g., days, night, weekends)?

_____

_____

_____

Do you plan to work with partners?

_____

_____

_____

What skills or finances will your partners bring to the table?

_____

_____

_____

Is there anything else you would like a mentor to know about?

_____

_____

_____

_____

****

Congratulations! You've just taken an incredible step towards your own personal growth by honestly evaluating where you are today. Nice work!

I guarantee any prospective mentor, who is committed to your success, will be able to help you maximize your growth, and success, based on your answers to these questions! So, keep it handy for future use!

And here's another thing. If you're planning to invest with other real estate professionals, these are great interview questions! They're also excellent if you are looking to hire your own team members.

If you'd like immediate feedback from a professional real estate mentor please feel free to send your completed Real Estate Investor Assessment and Questionnaire to:
theresa@theresabradleybanta.com

Let's figure out where you are right now, where your gaps in ability are and what you need to do to make this a reality.

I'll be happy to help you decide what steps you can take today to get your real estate business started. I offer a *free* 30-minute strategy session to help you plan your next step in your career as a multifamily real estate investor.

Complete the info below (your name, address, email and phone) and email it to theresa@theresabradleybanta.com so I'll know how to get in contact with you.

Name: _____

Date: _____

Address: _____

Home Phone: _____

Cell Phone: _____

Email: _____

Occupation: _____

To your real estate investing success!

Theresa Bradley-Banta
www.theresabradleybanta.com

If you'd like more information about my Investing in Residential and Multifamily Real Estate Mentoring & Consultancy Programs visit: www.theresabradleybanta.com/services.

Appendix B: Money Rules For Real Estate Investing

As you read my book **Invest In Apartment Buildings** *Profit Without The Pitfalls*, you heard me talk about Money Rules. I mentioned that in every business I've owned and in each investment I've made—whether in real estate, stocks, oil & gas, funds, start up businesses, or in other people's investment opportunities—I set a certain investment criteria and I don't deviate.

Without firm money rules you can find yourself being tempted by every bright shining object presented to you, whether or not they meet your investment criteria. You'll end up doing deals you're not 100% sure about. You can find your carefully laid out plans and strategies in shatters.

The form below can be used to start a list of your own money rules to help keep you on track. It's easier to say "No" to opportunities that present themselves to you when they don't meet your criteria.

Here's a reminder from the book. Your personal rules might also include things like:

- The type of return you need to get to do a deal (ROI, or return on investment).
- The price range you want to buy in.
- Your holding period (including flips if you decide to go that route).
- Your exit strategies (will you hold, re-finance or sell?)
- How much of your net worth you'll invest.
- Whether or not you want partners.
- How much of your personal time you're willing to devote

to your investing.

Your rules will be your own. No two people will have the same money rules. Here's a couple money rules to get you started (some of my favorites). Add your own rules to the rest of the list.

1. Everything's negotiable!

2. Always make money on the front end of the deal.

3. I won't do a deal without education and mentorship from successful multifamily investors.

4. My broker works for me—it's not the other way around.

5. I will never, ever fall in love with an investment property before I buy it.

6. Always (always, always!) get the Seller's numbers when I analyze a deal.

7. _____

8. _____

9. _____

10. _____

11. _____

12. _____

13. _____

14. _____

15. _____

16. _____

17. _____

18. _____

19. _____

20. _____

21. _____

22. _____

23. _____

24. _____

25. _____

26. _____

27. _____

Appendix C: Commercial Broker Interview Questions

1. Do you invest in property?

2. Do you consider that to be a conflict of interest?

    a. What happens when deals are first listed at your company? Do your brokers and principals have first crack at them?
    b. How do I get on your priority investor list?

3. Are you investor focused?

4. What markets do you work in? What can you tell me about them?

5. Can you provide the following research?

    a. Rent comparables. (Including concessions—economic and actual).
    b. Sold comparables (not just hand picked—*all* comps).
    c. Information on your current listings? What do you know about each property? It's history? It's location?
    d. Who bought the property? Who brokered the deal?
    e. Company multifamily market research.
    f. Capitalization rate trends: today and historical.
    g. Average property expenses ratios.

6. What stage is the market in? (10 year historicals)

    a. Emerging market? Recovering market? Etc.

7. Who is financing local deals?

8. What deals are not getting done?

9. What submarkets should I avoid? (Submarket level data— get it!)

10. What types of properties are in your favorite markets?

   a. Style, age, condition, upgrades, class, building materials, etc.

11. Tell me about local apartment inventory (supply and demand to forecast future markets for investment).

12. What do you know about shadow markets (non-apartment rentals)? How will they affect local multifamily markets?

13. Do you "buy" listings? A.K.A. unrealistic property prices just to get the listing.

14. Who has done really well? (your clients)

   a. When did they buy (year)? Review at least 10 years investment historicals.
   b. When did they sell? Review at least 10 years investment historicals.
   c. What were their strategies?
   d. What is the current investor demand for properties? (Less investor demand equals lower prices, higher caps.)

15. How many Buyer inquiries do you get in a week?

16. What were your sales for the past year and what was your average sale?

17. Why should I buy from/list with you rather than any other broker?

18. Will you give me your opinion of what the market value of a particular property is based on:

   a. Sold listings (comps)?
   b. Rent comps.
   c. Market stage (Emerging, over heated —Recovery, Expansion, Oversupply, Recession).
   d. Financial analysis?
   e. Will you provide the seller's actual #s before I consider making an offer on a deal?

19. Who do you recommend for:

   a. Mentors?
   b. Lenders?
   c. Inspectors?
   d. Property managers?
   e. Title company?
   f. Attorneys?
   g. Tax professionals?
   h. Rehabbers?
   i. Vendors (apartment market)?

20. Tell me about recent local apartment deals that have closed:

    a. Your deals.

    b. Other broker's deals.

Appendix D: Property Manager Interview Questions

1. How many properties do you manage?

    a. Location? Can I tour the properties?
    b. How many owners do you represent?
    c. Do you have references I can call?
    d. Unhappy past owners?
    e. Happy current owners?
    f. What's your current occupancy at all properties? What is your occupancy history?

2. Do you use on-site managers?

    a. At what properties? Why?
    b. What are their day-to-day responsibilities?
    c. How are they paid?
    d. When would you not use an on-site manager?
    e. Who manages the on-site manager?

3. What are your fees?

    a. What % of revenue do you charge?
    b. What do you charge for property renovation (if any)?
    c. What are your leasing fees?
    d. What are your maintenance fees?

4. How do you advertise and market your properties?

5. Where do you advertise and market your properties?

6. What are your accounting practices?

    a. What management /accounting software do you use?
    b. Mac friendly? (Important to know if *you* are Macintosh based.)
    c. What are the features?
    d. As an owner, can I access the data?
    e. Do you do a cash flow analysis?
    f. Will you complete a forecast vs. actual budget for my property?

7. What type of management reports do you provide?

    a. How frequently will I get property updates?

8. Do you file reports, receipts, invoices, leases, etc., for my property at your place of business?

9. Who does the books?

10. Will you assist with asset management and capitalization?

    a. Do you provide operations consulting?
    b. Does that include exit strategies?

11. Do you have experience with value added strategies?

12. Who are your contacts in the industry?

    a. Brokers?
    b. Lenders?

c. Vendors and service providers to the apartment industry?

13. Do you know of available properties for sale?

14. What is your background?

   a. Number of years in business?
   b. Any experience as an owner operator?
   c. Who is on your team? Are you replaceable? What happens if you have a personal emergency that takes you away from your business?

15. Tell me about your practices for resident relations:

   a. Late fees and collections?
   b. Leases vs. MTM (month-to-month)?
   c. Do you have repositioning experience?
   d. Tell me about your follow-up with resident maintenance requests.
   e. What are your rental techniques & property promotion strategies?
   f. Do you build community?
   g. How do you feel about good communication at the property?

Appendix E: Apartment Building Due Diligence Checklist

Most due diligence checklists out there in the market are extensive and contain a vast list of items you might request from a prospective seller of an apartment complex. The lists are almost a caricature of themselves. I mean, they have so many items that a seller and/or a broker will look at you as if you were nuts if you asked for everything on the list.

You will find two lists here. The first list is the stuff you should always request copies of (and in most cases expect to get). The second list contains items you'll want to ask for, but you may not always get copies from the seller—sometimes the seller doesn't have copies and/or they might not exist.

Some documents will be included in the Commercial Contract to Buy and are mandatory. For example, a request for a copy of evidence of title (owner's title insurance policy) and a property survey are standard inclusions on most commercial contracts. Read your local Contract to Buy and Sell Commercial Real Estate and become familiar with all obligations of the seller and the buyer for multifamily transactions.

You can include a request for any of the following documents in an addendum to your purchase contract. In other words, you can make receiving copies of particular documents a requirement of doing the deal. This can become a part of your inspection contingency meaning the contract is contingent upon your approval of both the physical inspection of the property and your approval of the documents.

Here's the list of due diligence items you should always request (and expect zero push back on):

1. A completed and signed Seller's Property Disclosure.

2. Copies of all leases and rental applications, to include:

   a. Most recent financial statements and credit information and reports, if any, on any tenant and of any guarantors of any leases or rents.
   b. Any executed letters of intent with prospective tenants, including lease concessions.
   c. Leasing status report from the leasing broker, including pending rental applications.
   d. Include copies of leases for all subsidized tenants and documents relating to any inspections by government agencies.

3. Historical rent delinquency reports.

4. Operating statements (income and expenses) for the previous two years of ownership *and* current year-to-date operating statements.

5. Certified rent roll showing unit numbers, tenant names, rent rates, security deposit amounts, current rent payment status and lease expiration dates.

6. A schedule of all capital improvements made to the property for the past 2-4 years.

7. Security deposit detail (tenants and pets).

8. All service contracts, manufacturer and service warranties and other written contracts or agreements. A property may have contracted services for: Laundry, pest control, trash hauling, landscaping, snow removal, elevator servicing, cleaning ser-

vices, window washing, security services, parking lot sweeping, etc. If possible obtain copies of current service contracts and review the following:

    a. Term of contract.
    b. Monthly cost for services.
    c. Work to be performed.
    d. Termination penalty.

9. As-built surveys showing any improvements to the property.

10. Copies of liens or liabilities on the property that should be known to the buyer prior to closing.

11. Copies of all insurance policies.

12. Copies of all insurance claims *in the past 5 years.*

13. Lead based paint disclosure.

14. Inventory of all property owned by the seller and a complete list of all inventory to be transferred with the property.

15. Physical inspection of the property (this is not a document—it's just a reminder that you should always request a physical inspection as part of your due diligence).

Here are additional due diligence documents that may be included in your document requests:

1. Names and contact information for all employees including salary information.

2. Copies of all warranties.

3. Copies of last two years' tax bills including evidence

of payment.

4. Copies of all architectural renderings and blueprints.

5. Environmental audits and reports.

6. Soils test reports.

7. Engineering studies including reports on walls, roofs, foundation, supports and floors.

8. Any structural, mechanical, electrical, plumbing, seismographic, HVAC or other property systems replacement, maintenance and/or repairs (including invoices and estimates).

9. Copy of current mortgage, and letter from current lender(s) showing the current balances and terms of the mortgages.

10. Copies of all local utility invoices showing current service.

11. Current operating and capital budgets of the Property, including comparison of actual to budgeted results and an explanation of significant variances.

12. Current aged receivables and payables reports.

13. Reports showing compliance with ADA requirements (Americans with Disabilities Act).

14. Building square footage certification.

15. Recent photographs of the property.

16. Copies of rental unit floor plans.

17. All property licenses and permits.

18. Certification of fire inspections and any other city sanctioned property inspections.

19. Certificates of occupancy for each tenant.

Appendix F: Team Member Checklist & Contact Information

Use this document as a checklist to be certain you have every member of your multifamily real estate investing team lined up. These are the professionals you should be able to contact at a moments notice—be sure to include their contact information!

Multifamily Investing Mentor(s)

Name: _____

Company: _____

Address: _____

_____

Office Phone: _____

Mobile: _____

Fax: _____

Website: _____

Commercial Real Estate Broker(s)

Name: _____

Company: _____

Address: _____

_____

Office Phone: _____

Mobile: _____

Fax: _____

Website: _____

Multifamily Property Manager

Name: __ _____

Company: _____

Address:_____

_____

Office Phone:_____

Mobile: _____

Fax: _____

Website: _____

Multifamily Property Inspector(s)

Name: _____

Company: _____

Address:_____

_____

Office Phone:_____

Mobile: _____

Fax: _____

Website: _____

Multifamily Property Inspector(s) - Engineer

Name: _____

Company: _____

Address:_____

_____

Office Phone:_____

Mobile: _____

Fax: _____

Website: _____

Rehab/Maintenance (contractors)

Name: _____

Company: _____

Address:_____

_____

Office Phone:_____

Mobile: _____

Fax: _____

Website: _____

Insurance

Name: _____

Company: _____

Address:_____

_____

Office Phone:_____

Mobile: _____

Fax: _____

Website: _____

Service providers and vendors (companies such as: trash, roofing, concrete/asphalt, pest control, cleaning, painting, carpeting, wood flooring, appliances, tile, boiler, electric, plumbing, laundry, sewer, windows/glass, landscaping)

Name: _____

Company: _____

Address:_____

_____

Office Phone:_____

Mobile: _____

Fax: _____

Website:_____

Commercial Lender(s)

Name: _____

Company: _____

Address:_____

_____

Office Phone:_____

Mobile: _____

Fax: _____

Website:_____

Title Company

Name: _____

Company: _____

Address:_____

_____

Office Phone:_____

Mobile: _____

Fax: _____

Website: _____

Attorney

Name: _____

Company: _____

Address: _____

_____

Office Phone: _____

Mobile: _____

Fax: _____

Website: _____

1031 Exchanger

Name: _____

Company: _____

Address: _____

_____

Office Phone: _____

Mobile: _____

Fax: _____

Website: _____

Tax Professional (CPA, Bookkeeper)

Name: _____

Company: _____

Address:_____

_____

Office Phone:_____

Mobile: _____

Fax: _____

Website:_____

Equity Partners (partners in your deal)

Name: _____

Company: _____

Address:_____

_____

Office Phone:_____

Mobile: _____

Fax: _____

Website:_____

Appendix G: Sample Real Estate Investor Resume

**Statement of Real Estate
Investor Experience For:**

Bryce Jones
ABC Real Estate Investments, LLC
1234 Main Street
Anytown, USA

p: 555.555.5555
f: 555.555.5551
email: byrce@g_mail.com

Bryce Jones is an experienced real estate investor. His investing experience includes single and multifamily real estate, and land development. His current focus is on multifamily real estate / apartments, education and acquisition of multifamily units.

Real estate experience:

1. Qualified Real Estate Professional under IRS guidelines.
2. Owns and operates a professional real estate management & investment company; duties include but are not limited to:
    a. Profit & Loss Statements, Balance Sheets.
    b. Bookkeeping.

    c. Forecasts.

    d. Property acquisition, rehab, marketing & sales.

    e. Property management and leasing.

3. Experienced in owning and managing SFRs & small multi-unit properties.

    a. Properties in New York, Pennsylvania, Arizona and Mexico.

    b. Properties include buy & holds, flips, land, re-fi's and short sales.

4. Instrumental in creating and currently operating Advisory Committee and Home Owners Association (HOA) for land development project in Scottsdale, AZ.

5. Multifamily Experience:

    a. Owner / operator of two multifamily properties.

    b. Extensive national market research & knowledge.

    c. Expert in multiple national submarkets.

       • Rents, cap rates, market values, vacancies, market cycles, etc.

    d. Extensive education and practical application in multifamily deal analysis.

    e. Direct marketing to owners – includes offers & contracts.

    f. Has local teams to stabilize properties, including management, rehabilitation and maintenance.

    g. Preparation of offering memorandums, deal structuring & finance.

6. Team members include (but are not limited to):

    a. Commercial property management company (AMC Apartment Management Co., contact: Ed Worth, 555-555-5555).

    b. Real estate attorney John Doe, partner in previous deals.

c. Raleigh Rehab, LLC. Scott Raleigh 555-555-5555.

References on request.

Appendix H: Sample Property Management Agreement

Apartment Management Agreement

This Apartment Management Agreement (the "Agreement") is made this _____ Day of September 2009 by and between _____ _____ ("Agent"), and ABC Apartment Investors, LLC ("Owner").

1) PROPERTY - That certain property consisting of the multifamily apartment complex known as _____ located at _____ in the city of _____, County of _____, State of _____ together with all personal property of Owner attached thereto, located thereon or used in connection therewith (The "Property").

2) AGENCY - In consideration of the property management services to be rendered by Agent pursuant to this Agreement, Owner hereby designates Agent as the exclusive Agent and representative of Owner for the purposes of management and operation for Owner's account of The Property.

3) TERM - This Agreement shall become effective as of the ___ day of _____ 20__. (the "Effective Date") and, shall continue in full force for 36 months. This Agreement shall automatically renew for a term of twelve (12) months unless written notice is received by Agent, from Owner, a minimum of thirty (30) days prior to the expiration of the term. Either party shall have the right to terminate this agreement

by delivering written notice thirty (30) days prior to termination.

4) MANAGEMENT FEE - (a) The agent will be paid a fee of ____% of the monthly collected revenues from the Property. Revenues include rent, pass through costs to tenants, vending income, and forfeited security deposits applied to rent (excluding damages). Revenues do not include insurance proceeds or other revenue sources not listed above. Agent will be reimbursed for all expenses directly related to the management and leasing of the Property. The Agent will not be reimbursed for Agent's general office overhead and expenses. Projects including, but not limited to, property renovation, reconstruction, or damage recovery are outside the scope of the normal management fees and will require additional compensation to be agreed upon by all parties prior to initiation of work. (b). Upon signing a new tenant into a new term lease, the Agent will be paid a one-time fee of ___% of monthly rent per unit. (c). Upon signing a current tenant into a new term lease of 6 months or greater, the Agent will be paid a one-time fee of ___% of monthly rent per unit. (d). Agent will be paid $___/hour for maintenance performed at the property.

5) POWERS AND DUTIES OF AGENT - The Agent shall (a) use its best efforts to keep the Property rented by procuring tenants for the Property, (b) collect the rents and other income due the Owner on a timely basis, (c) deposit all income, including security deposits, in a separate Broker Account on behalf of Owner, (d) pay normal reoccurring operating expenses on a timely basis from the trust account, provided funds are available, (e) hire employees, vendors, contractors, and suppliers to provide services, materials, equipment, and supplies for the benefit of the Tenants and Property, (f) secure Owner's approval on any expense, other than normal reoccurring operating expenses, that exceed One Thousand Dollars ($1,000.00) except for

emergencies to protect property, health, or life, (g) enforce the tenants' lease obligations and rules and regulations, (h) provide monthly operating statements, (i) keep the Owner informed of any potential problems, hazards, and code violations existing at the property, and (j) perform other reasonable duties or tasks requested by the Owner.

6) DUTIES OF OWNER - Owner shall be responsible for providing funds, or causing funds to be provided, for the Operating Account to meet on a timely basis, the cash requirements of Agent for the proper operation of the Property. Owner agrees to review monthly financial statements for any errors or discrepancies within 120 days from the close of the respective month.

7) OWNER'S AGENT AND SECURITY DEPOSITS - Pursuant to _____ [state] Real Estate Commission requirements; all security deposits received from tenants are transferred to Owner and are not held by Agent, owner has full financial responsibility for return of the security deposit to tenants. Owner authorizes the Agent to return any deposit due the tenant from the Owner's operating account. Owner appoints Agent as the Owner's representative for service of legal notices affecting the property. Upon notice of any dispute from the tenant, Agent will not unreasonably withhold the Owner's true name and current mailing address.

8) INSURANCE OBLIGATIONS – (a) Owner shall obtain and keep in force adequate insurance against physical damage (e.g., fire with extended coverage endorsement, boiler and machines, etc.) and against liability for loss, damage or injury to property or persons which might arise out of the occupancy, management, operation or maintenance of the Property. Manager shall be covered as an additional insured on all liability insurance maintained with respect to the

Property. Said policies shall provide that notice of default or cancellation shall be sent to Manager as well as Owner. (b) Agent will procure and maintain insurance against the misfeasance, malfeasance, or non-feasance (errors and omissions) management of the Property, with limits of not more than One Million Dollars and with a deductible of not less than Five Thousand dollars.

9) OWNER'S INDEMNIFICATION - Owner hereby warrants and represents to Agent that it has the lawful and proper authority to employ Agent as provided herein. Except in the event of the negligence or willful misconduct of Agent, its officers, directors, employees, successors, assigns or other persons acting on behalf of Agent, Owner shall indemnify, defend, and hold Agent harmless from any and all costs, expenses, attorney's fees, suits, liabilities and damages from or connected with the operation or management of the Property by Agent or the performance or exercise of any obligation, power or authority herein or hereafter granted to Agent. Owner also agrees to hold harmless and defend Agent from any and all claims arising by reason of Agent's employment of any Property employee, including all costs of Agent's employment of any Property employee, including all costs of defense. Owner shall further indemnify Agent against, and hold it harmless from, all damages, claims, loss, cost or expense, including, without limitation, attorney's fees and costs arising out of defects in design or construction of the improvements in the Property or any breach of any legal duty or obligation which is by law or under this Agreement the responsibility of Owner.

10) ARBITRATION - Any controversy or claim arising out of or relating to the interpretation or application of any provision of this Agreement shall be settled by mediation and/or binding arbitration in accordance with the Commercial Rules of the American Arbitration

Association then in effect. Judgment upon the award rendered by the arbitrators may be entered in any court of competent jurisdiction. The arbitration shall be held in _____ (City), _____(State). The expenses of the arbitration shall be borne by each party to this Agreement as determined by the arbitrators, provided that each party to this Agreement shall pay for and bear the cost of its own experts, evidence, and legal counsel.

IN WITNESS WHEREOF, the parties have executed this Agreement the ___day of _____, 20___.

Owner: ABC Apartment Investors, LLC

Agent: _____

By: _____

By:_____

ABC Apartment Investors, LLC

Appendix I: Websites Mentioned in This Book

Theresa Bradley-Banta's site
www.theresabradleybanta.com

All of the exhibits, documents and forms used in this book and in the Appendix are available for (free) download at:
www.theresabradleybanta.com/bookdownloads

Craig's List
www.craigslist.org

Rent.com
www.rent.com

Red Capital Group
www.redcapitalgroup.com

Marcus & Millichap
www.marcusmillichap.com

Grubb & Ellis
www.grubb-ellis.com

CB Richard Ellis
www.cbre.com

BedBugReports.com
www.bedbugreports.com

The Bedbug Registry
www.bedbugregistry.com

The National Apartment Association
www.naahq.org

Gary G. Tharp, CCIM
www.garytharp.com

LinkedIn
www.linkedin.com

About the Author

Theresa Bradley-Banta, Founder, Theresa Bradley-Banta Real Estate Consultancy, is a business owner and entrepreneur who fell in love with real estate investing (apartment buildings in particular) in 2004. Since then, she has become one of the leading real estate consultants in the country. Ms. Bradley-Banta has successfully invested across the U. S. and outside of it and has used that knowledge to mentor others so they, too, can grow in wisdom and in wealth. Her website is one of the most popular in the field for real estate mentoring programs, free resources and articles on multifamily real estate investing.

Theresa Bradley-Banta is a Winner of the Stevie Award for Women in Business, Entrepreneur of the Year, Business Services.

In addition to real estate investing, consulting and mentoring she is a musician, award winning graphic artist and owner of multiple businesses. She and her husband Richard live in Colorado.

Resources

Here's a Surprise!

Did you know that you can get the *free* downloads from my book today? Yep. Sure can. Just visit the link below.

www.theresabradleybanta.com/bookdownloads

I'm giving away free content like:

- Interview questions for hiring a commercial property broker.
- Apartment building due diligence checklist.
- Sample real estate investor resume (your lender will want to see this).
- And more.

You'll find all of the documents and exhibits used in this book as well as the documents that are included in the Appendix. You'll even find a couple of bonus documents that are not included this book.

Made in the USA
Lexington, KY
15 May 2013